THE
HOT & SPICY
COOKBOOK

MORE THAN 175 TANTALIZING RECIPES
FROM AROUND THE WORLD

THE
HOT & SPICY
COOKBOOK

MORE THAN 175 TANTALIZING RECIPES
FROM AROUND THE WORLD

CRESCENT BOOKS
New York/Avenel, New Jersey

Recipes and photographs on the following pages
are the copyright of Merehurst Press:
3, Bottom and Right, 5, 6, 7, 8, 9, 10, 11, 12, 13, 14, 15, 16, 17,
18, 19, 20, 21, 22, 23, 24, 25, 26, 27, 28, 29, 30, 31, 32, 33, 34,
35, 36, 37, 38, 39, 40, 41, 42, 43, 44, 45, 46, 47, 48

ISBN 0 517 06721 8

This 1992 edition published by Crescent Books, distributed by
Outlet Book Company, Inc., a Random House Company,
40 Engelhard Avenue, Avenel, New Jersey 070 01.

Printed and bound in Italy

8 7 6 5 4 3 2 1

CREDITS

Contributing authors: Linda Fraser, Louise Steele

Photography by: Paul Grater, Alister Thorpe

Design by: Sara Cooper

Typeset by: Maron Graphics Ltd. Wembley., Walkergate Press Ltd., Hull

Color separation by: J. Film Process Ltd., Magnum Graphics Ltd.

HOT
AND SPICY

CHILES

Chiles belong to the capsicum family, as do sweet peppers, but there the relationship ends, for the fiery heat of the chile is in no way similar to its mild-flavored relation. Fresh chiles are now widely available and vary considerably in size, shape and heat factor. In principle, the fatter chiles tend to be more mild than the long, thin varieties, and the smaller the chile, the hotter its taste. Generally, the unripened, green chile is less fiery than when ripened and red. This is a useful guide to follow, but there are exceptions according to the variety, so it is wise to remember that all chiles, irrespective of color, shape and size, are hot, so use caution before adding them to a dish. Bear in mind that a little chile goes a long way, so add a small amount to begin with and gradually increase the quantity to your liking during cooking.

Take care when preparing chiles – the tiny, cream-colored seeds inside are the hottest part and, in general, are removed before using. Chiles contain a pungent oil which can cause an unpleasant burning sensation to eyes and skin, so it's a wise precaution to wear rubber gloves when handling chiles and to be sure not to touch your face or eyes during preparation. Cut off the stalk end, then split open the pod and scrape out seeds, using a pointed knife, and discard. Rinse pod thoroughly with cold running water and pat chile dry before chopping or slicing as required. Once this task is completed, always wash your hands, utensils and surfaces thoroughly with soapy water.

Dried red chiles are sold whole and can vary in size from 1/2-3/4 to 1-1/2-2 inches in length, so take this into account when using. If a recipe states small dried chiles, and you only have the larger ones, adapt and lessen the quantity accordingly, or to taste. Dried chiles are usually soaked in hot water for 1 hour before draining and removing seeds (as described above), unless a recipe states otherwise.

Dried red chiles, when ground, are used to make cayenne pepper and, combined with other spices and seasonings, also make chile and curry powder, and chile seasoning. They are also used in the making of hot-pepper sauce and chile sauces.

The Harissa spice mix, page 8, uses a large quantity of dried chiles and is very hot, so be forewarned! This is a favorite spice mix for many Middle Eastern dishes. Don't be tempted to add more Harissa than the recipe states, unless you are prepared for an extremely hot dish. A less fiery Harissa can be made simply by removing the seeds from soaked chiles before crushing chiles with other ingredients.

Green chiles are available canned. These are often seeded and peeled and taste pleasantly hot and spicy – ideal for adding to pizza toppings, sauces and taco fillings. Both red and green chiles also come pickled in jars (hot or mild/sweet) and can be found in delicatessens and ethnic food shops. Canned and pickled varieties should be drained and patted dry before using. Whether you seed the pickled type is up to you, just remember the seeds are the hottest part!

mustard. Dry mustard can be used as it is in cooking, or it may be mixed to a paste with a little cold or warm water. (For a nice rich mixture, why not try mixing it with a little cream or milk?) Once mixed it should be left at least 10 minutes to allow time for the flavors to develop. It is only when the powder is mixed with a liquid that the essential oils are released, giving mustard its pungency and sensation of heat. Remember that made mustard loses its pungency after a few hours. Jars of prepared mustards, once opened, need using within a few weeks as the flavor and color will deteriorate.

The variety of ready-prepared mustards come in a bewildering number of mouthwatering flavors, according to the manufacturer. These can be made from milled mustard flour, or from coarsely crushed seed (the proportions of which vary tremendously, depending on the type). Some are mixed with vinegar, others with grape juice or wine (and sometimes beer), and often contain various spices, herbs and seasonings, such as honey and horseradish. German mustard, which is mild and sweet-flavored, is a mixture of brown and white mustard flour moistened with vinegar and flavored with various spices. The mild-flavored American mustard (popular with children) generally uses only yellow mustard seeds with the addition of sugar, vinegar and salt. Dijon-style mustard, made from milled, husked black seeds, is flavored with wine and spices. The pungent and spicy grainy types of mustard are a mixture of whole, crushed black and yellow seeds with additional flavorings added for individuality.

Mustards of all types can be used to great effect, not only as a condiment, but also as a culinary ingredient. They add bite and piquancy to all types of savory dishes from scrambled eggs, sauces and dressings to deviled mixtures, barbecued food, soups, casseroles, pastry, scones and cheesy biscuits.

MUSTARD

White or yellow, brown and black seeds come from the mustard plant, according to the species. Most commonly found is the creamy yellow type which is the least pungent. The brown type (or Indian mustard) is stronger in flavor, while the black mustard seed is the most powerful of all. The creamy yellow seeds are more widely available, but look for the black and brown types in Asian and Oriental food shops and delicatessens.

Whole mustard seeds have a pleasant nutty bite to them and can be used to add piquancy to salad dressing and hot sauces. They are especially good when served with fish, chicken and pork and are also delicious added to coleslaw, creamy potato salads, pickles and chutneys. Use mustard seeds (especially the two hotter varieties) with discretion to begin with, increasing the amount as you become more familiar with the flavors.

It is the yellow seed which, when processed with black seeds, wheat flour and turmeric, forms the basis of English

ALLSPICE (1): These small dark, reddish-brown berries are so called because their aroma and flavor resemble a combination of cinnamon, cloves and nutmeg. Use berries whole in marinades; for boiling and pot roasting meats and poultry; in fish dishes, pickles and chutneys. Also available ground and excellent for flavoring soups, sauces and desserts.

ANISE (2): Commonly called aniseed, these small, brown oval seeds have the sweet, pungent flavor of licorice. Also available ground. Use seeds in stews and vegetable dishes, or sprinkle over loaves and rolls before baking. Try ground anise for flavoring fish dishes and pastries for fruit pies.

CARAWAY (3): Small brown, crescent-shaped seeds with a strong liquorice flavor and especially delicious as a flavoring in braised cabbage and sauerkraut recipes, breads (particularly rye), cakes and cheeses.

CARDAMOM (4): Small, triangular-shaped pods containing numerous small black seeds which have a warm, highly aromatic flavor. You can buy green or black cardamoms although the smaller green type is more widely available.

CAYENNE (5): Orangey-red in color, this ground pepper is extremely hot and pungent. Not to be confused with paprika which, although related, is mild-flavored.

CHILE POWDER (6): Made from dried red chiles. This red powder varies in flavor and hotness, from mild to hot. A less fiery type is found in chile seasoning.

CINNAMON (7) & CASSIA (8): Shavings of bark from the cinnamon tree are processed and curled to form cinnamon sticks. Also available in ground form. Spicy, fragrant and sweet, it is used widely in savory and sweet dishes. Cassia (from the dried bark of the cassia tree) is similar to cinnamon, but less delicate in flavor with a slight pungent 'bite'.

CLOVES (9): These dried, unopened flower buds give a warm aroma and pungency to foods, but should be used with care as the flavor can become overpowering. Available in ground form. Cloves are added to soups, sauces, mulled drinks, stewed fruits and apple pies.

CORIANDER (10): Available in seed and ground form. These tiny, pale brown seeds have a mild, spicy flavor with a slight orange peel fragrance. An essential spice in curry dishes, but also extremely good in many cake and cookie recipes.

CUMIN (11): Sold in seed or ground. Cumin has a warm, pungent aromatic flavor and is used extensively to flavor curries and many Middle Eastern and Mexican dishes. Popular in Germany for flavoring sauerkraut and pork dishes. Use ground or whole in meat dishes and stuffed vegetables.

FENUGREEK (12): These small, yellow-brown seeds have a slight bitter flavor which, when added in small quantities, is very good in curries, chutneys and pickles, soups, fish and shellfish dishes.

GINGER (13): Available in many forms. Invaluable for adding to many savory and sweet dishes and for baking gingerbread and brandy snaps. Fresh ginger root looks like a knobby stem. It should be peeled and finely chopped or sliced before use. Dried ginger root is very hard and light beige in color. To release flavor, "bruise" with a spoon or soak in hot water before using. This dried type is more often used in pickling, jam making and preserving. Also available in ground form, preserved stem ginger and crystallized ginger.

MACE (14) & NUTMEG (15): Both are found on the same plant. The nutmeg is the inner kernel of the fruit. When ripe, the fruit splits open to reveal bright red arils which lie around the shell of the nutmeg – and once dried are known as mace blades. The flavor of both spices is very similar — warm, sweet and aromatic, although nutmeg is more delicate than mace. Both spices are also sold ground. Use with vegetables; sprinkled over egg dishes, milk puddings and custards; eggnogs and mulled drinks; or use as a flavoring in desserts.

PAPRIKA (16): Comes from a variety of pepper (capsicum) and although similar in color to cayenne, this bright red powder has a mild flavor.

PEPPER (17): White pepper comes from ripened berries with the outer

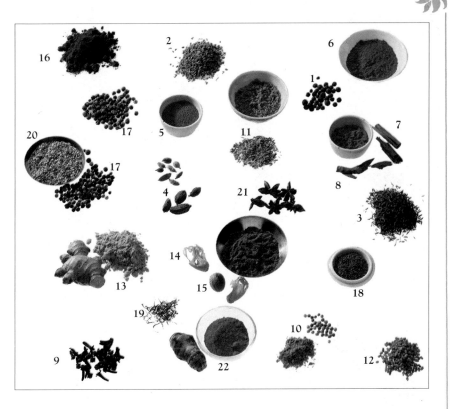

husks removed. Black pepper comes from unripened berries dried until dark greenish-black in color. Black pepper is more subtle than white. Use white or black peppercorns in marinades and pickling, or freshly ground as a seasoning. Both are available ground. Green peppercorns are also unripe berries with a mild, light flavor. They are canned in brine or pickled, or freeze-dried in jars. They add a pleasant, light peppery flavor to sauces, pâtés and salad dressings. Drain those packed in liquid and use either whole or mash them lightly before using. Dry green peppercorns should be lightly crushed before using to help release flavor, unless otherwise stated in a recipe.

POPPY SEEDS (18): These tiny, slate-blue seeds add a nutty flavor to both sweet and savory dishes. Sprinkle over desserts and breads.

SAFFRON (19): This spice comes from the stigmas of a species of crocus. It has a distinctive flavor and gives a rich yellow coloring to dishes, however, it is also the most expensive spice to buy. Available in small packets or jars (either powdered or in strands – the strands being far superior in flavor). This spice is a must for an authentic paella or Cornish Saffron Cake. Also an extremely good flavoring for soups, fish and chicken dishes.

SESAME SEEDS (20): High in protein and mineral oil content, sesame seeds have a crisp texture and sweet, nutty flavor which combines well in curries and with chicken, pork and fish dishes. Use also to sprinkle over breads, cookies and pastries before baking.

STAR ANISE (21): This dried, star-shaped seed head has a pungent, aromatic smell, rather similar to fennel. Use very sparingly in stir-fry dishes. Also good with fish and poultry.

TURMERIC (22): Closely related to ginger, it is an aromatic root which is dried and ground to produce a bright, orange-yellow powder. It has a rich, warm, distinctive smell, a delicate, aromatic flavor and helps give dishes an attractive yellow coloring. Use in curries, fish and shellfish dishes, rice pilafs and lentil mixtures. It is also a necessary ingredient in mustards, pickles and piccalilli.

All spices should be stored in small airtight jars in a cool, dark place, as heat, moisture and sunlight reduce their flavor.

SPICE MIXTURES

GARAM MASALA

10 green or 6 black cardamoms, pods cracked, seeded
1 tablespoon black peppercorns
2 teaspoons cumin seeds
½ teaspoon coriander seeds
2 small dried red chiles, seeded

Using a blender, process all ingredients until finely ground. Store in an airtight jar up to 3 months.

CURRY POWDER

2 tablespoons cumin seeds
2 tablespoons fenugreek
1-½ teaspoons mustard seeds
1 tablespoon black peppercorns
½ cup coriander seeds
1 tablespoon poppy seeds
1 tablespoon ground ginger
1-½ teaspoons hot chile powder
¼ cup ground turmeric

Using a blender, process cumin, fenugreek, mustard, peppercorns, coriander and poppy seeds. Add remaining spices; process. Store up to 3 months.

FIVE SPICE POWDER

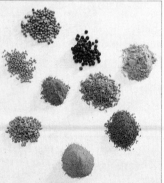

5 teaspoons ground anise (aniseed)
5 teaspoons star anise
1 (5-inch) cinnamon stick or equivalent in cassia bark
2 tablespoons whole cloves
7 teaspoons fennel seeds

Using a blender, process all ingredients until finely ground. Store in an airtight jar up to 3 months.

MIXED SPICE

1 (3-inch) cinnamon stick, broken in small pieces
2-½ teaspoons allspice berries
1 tablespoon whole cloves
2 teaspoons freshly grated nutmeg
1 tablespoon ground ginger

Using a coffee grinder or blender, process cinnamon, allspice berries and cloves until very finely ground. Add to freshly grated nutmeg and ginger and mix well. Store in a small, airtight jar up to 1 month.

PICKLING SPICE

2 tablespoons mace blades
1 tablespoon allspice berries
1 tablespoon whole cloves
2 (3-inch) cinnamon sticks, broken into small pieces
12 black peppercorns
1 dried bay leaf, crumbled

In a small bowl, mix all ingredients. Store in a small, airtight jar up to 2 months.

HARISSA

1 ounce dried red chiles
1 clove garlic, chopped
1 teaspoon caraway seeds
1 teaspoon cumin seeds
1 teaspoon coriander seeds
Several pinches salt
Olive oil

Soak chiles in hot water 1 hour. Drain well; pat dry. Grind to a smooth paste with garlic, spices and salt. Add enough olive oil to cover surface. Cover and store in a cool place up to 2 months.

—MARINATED SPICED OLIVES—

BOMBAY NUT 'N' RAISIN MIX—

¾ cup pitted ripe olives
¾ cup pimento-stuffed green olives
3 lemon slices
3 dried red chiles
2 garlic cloves, crushed
1 teaspoon mustard seeds
1 teaspoon black peppercorns
3 allspice berries
About 1-¾ cups olive oil

Drain any brine from olives. Put olives into a bowl.

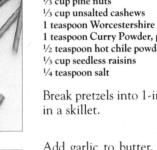

⅔ cup thin pretzel sticks
3 tablespoons butter
1 clove garlic, crushed
⅓ cup unblanched almonds
⅓ cup pine nuts
⅓ cup unsalted cashews
1 teaspoon Worcestershire sauce
1 teaspoon Curry Powder, page 8
½ teaspoon hot chile powder
⅓ cup seedless raisins
¼ teaspoon salt

Break pretzels into 1-inch sticks. Melt butter in a skillet.

Add lemon slices, chiles, garlic, mustard seeds, peppercorns and allspice berries. Stir in olive oil and mix well. Spoon mixture into a large jar with a tight-fitting lid. Screw on lid tightly and turn jar over several times to ensure ingredients are well mixed.

Add garlic to butter, then stir in almonds, pine nuts and cashews. Add Worcestershire sauce, curry powder and chile powder and mix well. Stir in pretzels and cook gently over medium heat 3 to 4 minutes, stirring frequently.

Let olives marinate at least 1 week before serving, turning jar several times a day. Store up to 6 months in a cool place.

Makes 4 to 6 servings.

NOTE: Use a mixture of corn oil and olive oil for a more economical marinade. Add sprigs of dried herbs to marinade, if desired. To serve, garnish with lemon twists and a fresh parsley sprig, if desired.

Remove from heat. Add raisins and salt; mix well. Turn mixture into a serving dish and cool.

Makes about 2 cups.

FILO SHRIMP PUFFS

1 tablespoon sesame oil
2 tablespoons corn oil
1 clove garlic, crushed
1 onion, finely chopped
1 (1-inch) piece ginger root, peeled, grated
1/2 teaspoon turmeric
1/2 teaspoon chile powder
1/4 teaspoon ground cumin
6 ounces medium-size peeled raw shrimp, thawed
  if frozen
2 tablespoons creamed coconut, diced
5 sheets filo pastry
1/4 cup butter or ghee, melted
Fresh Italian parsley sprigs, if desired

Preheat oven to 350F (175C). Lightly grease a baking sheet. Heat sesame and corn oil in a saucepan. Add garlic, onion and ginger. Fry gently 5 minutes, stirring occasionally.

Add turmeric, chile powder and cumin. Fry gently 2 minutes. Add shrimp, cover and cook gently 5 minutes, stirring frequently. Remove from heat, stir in creamed coconut and cool.

Work with 1 to 2 sheets of filo pastry at a time; cover remainder with a damp cloth. Cut sheet of pastry in half lengthwise and then fold each piece in half lengthwise to make 2 long narrow strips. Spoon a portion of shrimp mixture in 1 corner of each strip of pastry. Brush pastry all over with a small amount of melted butter or ghee.

Fold pastry and filling over at right angles to make a triangle. Continue folding in this way along pastry strip to form a triangular parcel. Brush with melted butter or ghee and place on greased baking sheet. Repeat with remaining pastry and shrimp mixture.

Bake in preheated oven 20 minutes. Brush with remaining melted butter or ghee and return to oven 5 to 10 minutes or until puffs are golden brown. Garnish with parsley sprigs, if desired, and serve warm.

Makes 10 puffs.

TANGY POTTED CHEESE

CHEESE CHILE BITES

4 ounces Cheddar cheese
¼ cup butter, softened
1 tablespoon port or sherry
4 green onions, finely chopped
½ teaspoon caraway seeds
½ to 1 teaspoon coarsely ground mustard
¼ teaspoon Worcestershire sauce
¼ cup walnuts, coarsely chopped
Crackers or melba toast
Fresh parsley sprigs, if desired

Finely grate cheese into a bowl. Add butter and mix well.

Stir in port, green onions, caraway seeds, mustard and Worcestershire sauce. Mix thoroughly until well combined.

Spoon mixture into a serving dish. Cover with walnuts and press walnuts down lightly into mixture. Chill at least 2 hours. Serve with crisp crackers or Melba toast and garnish with parsley sprigs, if desired.

Makes 4 to 6 servings.

Variation: Add 1 teaspoon chopped fresh herbs and a few pinches cayenne pepper to taste.

NOTE: This spread will keep in refrigerator up to 5 days.

1 cup all-purpose flour
¼ teaspoon salt
½ teaspoon dry mustard
¼ to ½ teaspoon hot chile powder
Large pinch cayenne pepper
¼ cup butter or margarine
½ cup (2 oz.) finely grated Cheddar cheese
1 egg, beaten
1 tablespoon cold water
1 tablespoon sesame seeds
1 tablespoon poppy seeds

Preheat oven to 400F (205C). Sift flour, salt and spices into a bowl.

Cut in butter finely until mixture resembles breadcrumbs. Add grated cheese and mix well. Mix egg with cold water. Add 2 tablespoons of egg mixture to cheese mixture and mix to form a fairly stiff dough. Knead gently on a lightly floured surface. Roll out dough to a 12″ × 6″ rectangle. Trim edges. Cut in half lengthwise and transfer to a baking sheet.

Brush each half with remaining egg mixture. Sprinkle 1 half with sesame seeds and the other half with poppy seeds. Cut each half in 10 triangles and separate slightly to prevent sticking. Bake in preheated oven 10 to 12 minutes or until light golden and cooked through. Cool on a wire rack. Store in an airtight container up to 2 weeks.

Makes 20 appetizers.

CURRIED CHICKEN LIVER PÂTÉ

¾ cup butter
1 onion, finely chopped
1 garlic clove, chopped
8 ounces chicken livers
1 to 2 teaspoons Curry Powder, page 8
½ cup chicken stock
2 hard-boiled eggs, shelled
Salt and freshly ground pepper to taste
2 pinches cayenne pepper
Fresh bay leaves, if desired
Lemon pieces, if desired
Crusty bread

Melt ½ of butter in a skillet. Add onion, garlic and chicken livers and cook gently 5 minutes, stirring constantly.

Stir in curry powder and cook 1 minute. Add chicken stock and cook gently 5 minutes, stirring and turning livers frequently. In a blender or food processor, process chicken liver mixture and hard-boiled eggs to a smooth purée.

Add salt, pepper and cayenne pepper. Turn mixture into a serving dish or terrine. Smooth surface. Melt remaining butter in a saucepan and pour over surface of pâté. Let set slightly, then garnish with bay leaves and lemon pieces, if desired. Chill several hours or overnight before serving with bread.

Makes 6 servings.

Variation: Add curry powder to taste to melted butter topping.

MUSSEL & SAFFRON SOUP

2 pounds mussels
1-¼ cups dry white wine
1-½ cups water
3 tablespoons butter
1 tablespoon olive oil
1 onion, finely chopped
1 garlic clove, crushed
1 leek, trimmed, finely shredded
½ teaspoon fenugreek, finely crushed
1-½ tablespoons all-purpose flour
2 (0.05 gram) packets saffron strands, soaked in
    1 tablespoon boiling water
1-¼ cups chicken stock
1 tablespoon chopped fresh parsley
Salt and freshly ground pepper to taste
2 tablespoons whipping cream
Fresh parsley sprigs, if desired

Scrub mussels clean in several changes of fresh water and pull off beards. Discard any mussels that are cracked or do not close tightly when tapped. Put mussels into a saucepan with wine and water. Cover and cook over high heat, shaking pan frequently, 6 to 7 minutes or until shells open. Remove mussels, discarding any which remain closed. Strain liquid through a fine sieve and reserve.

Heat butter and oil in a saucepan. Add onion, garlic, leek and fenugreek and cook gently 5 minutes. Stir in flour and cook 1 minute. Add saffron mixture, 2-½ cups of reserved cooking liquid and chicken stock. Bring to a boil, cover and simmer gently 15 minutes. Meanwhile, keep 8 mussels in shells and remove remaining mussels from shells. Add all mussels to soup and stir in chopped parsley, salt, pepper and cream. Heat through 2 to 3 minutes. Garnish with parsley sprigs, if desired, and serve hot.

Makes 4 servings.

CHILIED RED BEAN DIP

SPICED MELON COCKTAIL

2 tablespoons corn oil
1 clove garlic, crushed
1 onion, finely chopped
1 fresh green chile, seeded, finely chopped
1 teaspoon hot chile powder
1 (15-oz.) can red kidney beans
½ cup (2 oz.) shredded Cheddar cheese
Salt to taste
Thin slivers fresh red and green chiles
Fresh parsley sprig, if desired
Tortilla chips

Heat oil in a skillet. Add garlic, onion, green chile and chile powder and cook gently 4 minutes.

Drain kidney beans, reserving juice. Reserve 3 tablespoons beans; process remainder in a blender or food processor to a purée. Add to onion mixture and stir in 2 tablespoons of reserved bean liquid; mix well.

Stir in reserved beans and cheese. Cook gently about 2 minutes, stirring until cheese melts. Add salt and mix well. If mixture becomes too thick, add a little more reserved bean liquid. Spoon into a serving dish and garnish with chiles and parsley sprig, if desired. Serve warm with tortilla chips.

Makes 4 to 6 servings.

1 ripe honeydew melon, cut in half, seeded
1-½ cups whipping cream
1-½ cups mayonnaise
2 teaspoons lemon juice
1 teaspoon paprika
½ teaspoon hot-pepper sauce
½ teaspoon Worcestershire sauce
2 tablespoons tomato paste
8 ounces white crabmeat, flaked
8 radicchio leaves, shredded
Lemon and lime slices, if desired
Fresh mint sprigs, if desired

Scoop melon in balls.

To make dressing, whip cream until soft peaks form. Mix in mayonnaise, lemon juice, paprika, hot-pepper sauce, Worcestershire sauce and tomato paste.

Stir crabmeat into dressing. Lightly mix in melon and toss ingredients gently until coated. Arrange shredded radicchio on 4 individual serving dishes. Spoon melon and crab mixture to radicchio. Chill lightly. To serve, garnish with citrus slices and mint sprigs, if desired.

Makes 4 servings.

DEVILED TOMATOES

4 firm tomatoes
2 tablespoons butter
1 small clove garlic, crushed
½ cup fresh white bread crumbs
1 tablespoon chopped fresh parsley
¼ teaspoon cayenne pepper
½ teaspoon paprika
¼ teaspoon dry mustard
1 tablespoon grated Parmesan cheese
Salt to taste
Fresh parsley sprigs

Preheat oven to 350F (175C). Grease a 9-inch-square baking pan. Cut ⅓ slice off top of each tomato.

Reserve tops for 'lids'. Remove seeds from each tomato. Melt butter in a saucepan. Add garlic, bread crumbs and chopped parsley; mix well.

Remove from heat. Add cayenne pepper, paprika, mustard, cheese and salt; mix well. Spoon into tomatoes and form in neat mounds, pressing gently in shape with fingertips. Put reserved 'lids' on top. Arrange tomatoes, cut-sides up, in greased pan. Bake in preheated oven 15 minutes. Garnish with parsley sprigs and serve hot.

Makes 4 servings.

ORIENTAL GINGERED SHRIMP

8 unshelled raw jumbo shrimp, thawed if frozen
½ cup all-purpose flour
¼ teaspoon salt
1 teaspoon corn oil
¼ cup water
1 (1-inch) piece ginger root, peeled, grated
1 clove garlic, crushed
1 teaspoon chile sauce
1 egg white
Vegetable oil
1 green onion daisy
Red bell pepper strips

Shell shrimp, leaving tail shells on. Make a small incision along spines. Remove black spinal cord from shrimp.

In a bowl, combine flour, salt, corn oil and water. Stir in ginger, garlic and chile sauce and beat well. Stiffly whisk egg white, then gently fold into batter until evenly combined.

Half fill a deep-fat fryer or saucepan with oil; heat to 375F (190C) or until a ½-inch cube of day-old bread browns in 40 seconds. Hold each shrimp by its tail and dip into batter, then lower into hot oil. Fry 3 minutes or until golden. Drain on paper towels. Garnish with green onion daisy and bell pepper strips and serve hot.

Makes 4 servings.

CREOLE GUMBO POT

1 small eggplant
2 teaspoons salt
3 tablespoons olive oil
1 large onion, chopped
1 red pepper, seeded, diced
1 clove garlic, crushed
2 teaspoons paprika
½ teaspoon hot chile powder
4 ounces fresh okra
¾ cup frozen corn, thawed
2 cups boiling chicken stock
1 (8-oz.) can tomatoes in tomato juice
2 tablespoons long grain white rice
8 ounces peeled cooked medium-size shrimp, thawed
   if frozen
Salt and freshly ground pepper to taste
Fresh dill sprigs, if desired

Trim stalk end from eggplant. Cut in ½-inch pieces and place in a colander. Sprinkle with 2 teaspoons salt; let stand 30 minutes. Rinse under cold water and drain well.

Heat olive oil in a saucepan. Add eggplant, onion, red pepper and garlic and fry over low heat 5 minutes, stirring frequently. Stir in paprika and chile powder and cook gently 2 minutes.

Trim stalk ends from okra and discard. Cut okra in quarters.

Add okra, corn, chicken stock and tomatoes to eggplant mixture. Break up tomatoes with a spoon. Stir in rice, cover and simmer gently 25 minutes or until vegetables and rice are tender.

Add shrimp to mixture and heat through 5 minutes, stirring occasionally. Season with salt and pepper. Garnish with dill sprigs, if desired.

Makes 4 to 6 servings.

Variation: Stir in ⅔ cup half and half and heat through just before serving.

FRIED DEVILED CAMEMBERT

BARBECUED SPARERIBS

4 (1-½-oz.) pieces fairly firm Camembert cheese
2 teaspoons all-purpose flour
½ teaspoon dry mustard
½ teaspoon dried mixed herbs
Freshly ground pepper to taste
1 egg, beaten
¼ cup dry bread crumbs
½ teaspoon hot chile powder
3 to 4 pinches cayenne pepper
Vegetable oil for deep frying
Fresh sage, rosemary and thyme sprigs, if desired

Wrap and freeze cheese 1 hour.

2 pounds pork spareribs
2 tablespoons dark soy sauce
1 tablespoon tomato paste
2 good pinches Five Spice Powder, page 8
3 tablespoons honey
1 clove garlic, crushed
1 (½-inch) piece ginger root, peeled, grated
½ cup unsweetened orange juice
¼ teaspoon mustard powder
Orange peel, if desired

Preheat oven to 375F (190C). Cut ribs in single portions and arrange in a single layer in a roasting pan.

On a plate, combine flour, mustard, herbs and pepper. Dredge each piece of cheese thoroughly with mixture, then dip into egg. In a small bowl, mix bread crumbs with chile powder and cayenne pepper. Coat dipped cheese portions in mixture, pressing on firmly with palms of hands.

Mix remaining ingredients in a bowl until thoroughly combined. Spoon approximately ½ of sauce over ribs and bake in preheated oven 30 minutes.

Half fill a deep-fat fryer or saucepan with oil. Heat to 375F (190C) or until a ½-inch cube of day-old bread browns in 40 seconds. Fry cheese about 30 seconds or until golden brown. Drain on paper towels. Garnish with sage, rosemary and thyme sprigs, if desired, and serve at once.

Makes 4 servings.

Increase oven temperature to 400F (205C). Turn ribs and spoon remaining sauce over ribs. Bake 50 to 60 minutes, basting and turning frequently until ribs are glazed and rich golden brown. Garnish with orange peel, if desired, and serve hot.

Makes 4 servings.

GUACAMOLE

2 ripe avocados
1 tablespoon lemon juice
1 small clove garlic, if desired
1 small fresh green chile, seeded
1 shallot, finely chopped
1 tablespoon olive oil
Few drops hot-pepper sauce
Salt to taste
1 lemon slice, cut in pieces
Fresh Italian parsley sprig, if desired
Tortilla chips

Cut avocados in half, remove seeds and scoop flesh onto a plate. Mash well.

Add lemon juice and garlic, if desired, and mix well. Very finely chop chile and add to mixture with shallot.

Stir in olive oil, hot-pepper sauce and salt and mix well. Spoon mixture into a serving bowl and garnish with lemon pieces and parsley sprig, if desired. Serve with tortilla chips.

Makes 4 to 6 servings.

ANCHOVY SPREAD

1 (2-oz.) can anchovy fillets, drained
1 tablespoon milk
2 tablespoons butter, softened
1 ounce Bel Paese cheese
1 teaspoon lemon juice
3 pinches cayenne pepper
3 pinches ground nutmeg
¼ teaspoon hot-pepper sauce
2 teaspoons capers, drained, finely chopped
Hot toast strips
Radish slices
Watercress sprigs

Put anchovies into a bowl with milk. Let soak 30 minutes. Drain well, then pat anchovies dry with paper towels.

Chop anchovies finely and put into a bowl with butter and cheese; mix well. Add lemon juice, cayenne, nutmeg and hot-pepper sauce.

In a blender or food processor, process to a smooth purée scraping mixture from sides of bowl occasionally. Add capers and mix well. Spread thinly on toast. Garnish with radish slices and watercress.

Makes 4 to 6 servings.

NOTE: This mixture will keep in refrigerator up to 5 days.

SESAME SHRIMP TOASTS

6 ounces cooked peeled medium-size shrimp, thawed
   if frozen
1 (¾-inch) piece ginger root, peeled, grated
1 clove garlic, crushed
2 teaspoons cornstarch
1 egg white
3 pinches Five Spice Powder, page 8
Salt and freshly ground pepper to taste
4 thin slices white bread, crusts removed
3 tablespoons sesame seeds
Vegetable oil for shallow frying
Green onion daisies

Drain shrimp well on paper towels.

Mince shrimp finely. In a bowl, mix shrimp
with ginger, garlic and cornstarch. Lightly
whisk egg white with a fork (just enough to
make frothy) and add to shrimp. Stir in Five
Spice Powder, salt and pepper; mix well.

Press shrimp mixture evenly and firmly onto
slices of bread. Sprinkle with sesame seeds
and press on firmly. Heat ¾-inch oil in a
large skillet. Lower slices of bread, shrimp-
sides down, into hot oil and fry 2 to 3
minutes or until golden brown. Keep slices
immersed in oil. Drain on paper towels. Cut
into fingers and garnish with green onion
daisies. Serve hot.

Makes 4 servings.

MULLIGATAWNY SOUP

3 tablespoons butter
1 tablespoon corn oil
1 large onion, chopped
2 stalks celery, sliced thinly
3 carrots, diced
1-½ tablespoons Curry Powder, page 8
2 tablespoons all-purpose flour
5 cups chicken stock
2 tablespoons long grain white rice
2 tomatoes, peeled, chopped
8 ounces cooked chicken, diced
1 small cooking apple, peeled, cored, diced
Salt to taste
Fresh celery leaves, if desired
Carrot strip, if desired

Heat butter and oil in a saucepan.

Add onion, celery and carrots; cook gently 5
minutes. Stir in Curry Powder and flour and
cook 1 minute. Stir in stock and bring to a
boil; add rice and stir well.

Cover and simmer 20 minutes, stirring
occasionally. Add tomatoes, chicken, apple
and salt. Cover again and simmer 15
minutes. Garnish with celery leaves and
carrot strip, if desired, and serve hot.

Makes 4 servings.

BEEF SATAY

CURRY CREAM MUSSELS

3 tablespoons corn oil
1 small onion, finely chopped
1 clove garlic, crushed
1/2 teaspoon hot chile powder
1 to 1-1/2 teaspoons Curry Powder, page 8
1-1/4 cups water
2/3 cup crunchy peanut butter
1 teaspoon light-brown sugar
2 teaspoons dark soy sauce
1 teaspoon lemon juice
Salt and freshly ground pepper to taste
1 pound boneless sirloin steak
Lemon pieces, if desired
Fresh cilantro sprigs, if desired

2 pounds mussels, cleaned, page 12
2/3 cup water
2/3 cup dry cider
3 sprigs fresh thyme
1 clove garlic, crushed
2 tablespoons butter
3 shallots, finely chopped
1 stalk celery, finely chopped
1 tablespoon Curry Powder, page 8
1 tablespoon all-purpose flour
1/4 cup half and half
1/4 cup mayonnaise
Fresh dill sprigs, if desired
Hot crusty bread

To make peanut sauce, heat 2 tablespoons of oil in a saucepan. Add onion and garlic and fry gently until golden.

Stir in chile powder, Curry Powder, water, peanut butter and brown sugar. Bring to a boil; simmer gently until thickened. Stir in soy sauce and lemon juice, then salt and pepper. Turn mixture into a serving dish.

Place cleaned mussels in a saucepan with water, cider, thyme and garlic. Cover and cook over high heat, shaking pan frequently, 6 to 7 minutes or until shells open. Discard any mussels which remain closed. Cool mussels in liquid. Drain off cooled liquid, strain through a fine sieve and reserve. Discard thyme. Remove a half shell from each mussel and arrange mussels on 4 serving plates.

Preheat broiler. Grease a broiler pan. Trim and cut meat in 1/2-inch cubes. Thread (not too tightly) onto 8 bamboo skewers, leaving a space at each end for holding. Cover ends with small pieces of foil to prevent burning. Place skewers in greased broiler pan. Brush with remaining 1 tablespoon oil. Cook under preheated broiler 10 to 15 minutes until golden and cooked through. Turn and brush frequently with oil during cooking. Garnish with lemon pieces and cilantro sprigs, if desired, and serve hot with peanut sauce.

Melt butter in a saucepan. Add shallots and celery and cook gently 5 minutes. Add Curry Powder and flour and cook 1 minute. Stir in 1 cup of reserved liquid. Bring to a boil, stirring constantly. Cover and cook gently 10 minutes, stirring frequently. Cool. Stir in half and half and mayonnaise and mix well. Spoon sauce over mussels and garnish with dill sprigs, if desired. Serve with bread.

Makes 4 servings.

Makes 4 servings.

GADO GADO

8 ounces white cabbage
¼ cup sesame oil
1 large onion, cut in fourths, thinly sliced
1 green bell pepper, seeded, thinly sliced
6 ounces fresh bean sprouts
1 fresh green chile, seeded, finely chopped
1 clove garlic, crushed
2 shallots, finely chopped
½ teaspoon ground cumin
⅓ cup smooth peanut butter
3 tablespoons lemon juice
Few drops hot-pepper sauce
⅓ cup water
Red bell pepper strips, if desired

Finely shred cabbage, discarding stalk.

Heat 2 tablespoons of sesame oil in a skillet. Add cabbage, onion, thinly sliced bell pepper, bean sprouts and chile and fry over fairly high heat 3 to 4 minutes, stirring constantly. Remove from heat, spoon mixture into a serving dish; cool.

To make sauce, heat remaining sesame oil in saucepan. Add garlic, shallots and cumin and fry gently 5 minutes. Add peanut butter and cook gently 2 minutes. Stir in lemon juice, hot-pepper sauce and water and heat through gently to form a fairly thick sauce. Garnish sauce with bell pepper strips, if desired, and serve with cooled vegetables.

Makes 4 to 6 servings.

PEPPERED FARMHOUSE PÂTÉ

8 slices bacon
1 pound fresh pork picnic shoulder
12 ounces pork liver
1 onion, quartered
1 clove garlic
8 ounces veal cutlets
1 egg, beaten
1 teaspoon salt
2 teaspoons green peppercorns
1 teaspoon dried mixed herbs
2 tablespoons brandy
Additional green peppercorns, if desired
Fresh bay leaf, if desired
Crusty bread

Preheat oven to 350F (175C). Remove rinds and bones from bacon and pork.

Stretch bacon on a board using back of a knife until bacon is almost double in length. Line bottom and sides on a 5-cup terrine or soufflé dish with bacon. Mince shoulder pork, liver, onion and garlic. Cut veal in ½-inch pieces. In a bowl, combine pork shoulder, liver, veal, onion and garlic. Stir in egg, salt, peppercorns, herbs and brandy; mix thoroughly.

Spoon mixture into bacon-lined dish and smooth surface. Cover tightly with foil. Put into a roasting pan half filled with hot water. Bake in preheated oven 2 hours. Cool 30 minutes. Top with a plate and place a heavy weight on plate. Cool completely, then refrigerate overnight. Turn out onto a serving plate. Garnish with additional green peppercorns and bay leaf, if desired, and serve with bread.

Makes 8 servings.

ORANGE GINGER DUCKLING

TROPICAL FISH KEBABS

1 (4-lb.) oven-ready duckling
3 tablespoons corn oil
8 ounces Chinese pea pods, ends removed
3 stalks celery, sliced diagonally
12 green onions, sliced diagonally
1 red pepper, seeded, cut in small diamonds
1 (3-inch) piece ginger root, peeled, chopped
1 tablespoon granulated sugar
1 tablespoon soy sauce
1 tablespoon dry sherry
1 tablespoon malt vinegar
1 tablespoon tomato paste
2 teaspoons cornstarch
⅔ cup orange juice

Preheat oven to 350F (175C). Prick duckling skin all over with a fork and put into a roasting pan. Bake in preheated oven 1-¾ hours until golden and cooked; cool. Strip flesh and skin from carcass and cut in thin strips. Heat 2 tablespoons of oil in a large skillet or wok. Add pea pods and celery and stir-fry 2 minutes. Add green onions, red pepper and ginger and stir-fry 2 minutes. Remove from skillet and keep warm.

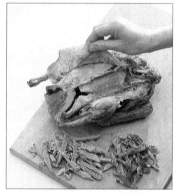

Heat remaining oil in skillet. Add duckling; stir-fry 2 minutes. Remove from skillet; keep warm. In a small bowl, mix sugar, soy sauce, sherry, vinegar and tomato paste. Blend cornstarch with a little orange juice, then stir in remaining juice. Add to soy sauce mixture. Pour into skillet; bring to a boil, stirring constantly. Reduce heat; simmer 2 minutes. Add vegetables and duckling to sauce and heat through.

Makes 4 servings.

NOTE: Serve with rice, garnished with orange pieces and Chinese snow peas, noodles and crisp shrimp crackers.

2 pounds monkfish
2 cloves garlic, crushed
1 fresh green chile, seeded, chopped
1 (1-inch) piece ginger root, peeled, chopped
Juice 1 lime
Salt and freshly ground pepper to taste
⅓ cup corn oil
1 ripe mango
2 bananas
1 red bell pepper, seeded, cut in cubes
Lime wedges

Cut away monkfish from central bone. Cut flesh in bite-size pieces.

In a shallow glass dish, combine garlic, chile, ginger, lime juice, salt, pepper and oil. Add fish and stir gently. Cover and refrigerate 2 hours. Meanwhile, slice mango lengthwise on each side, close to seed. Peel and cut mango flesh in small pieces. Preheat grill. Cut bananas in chunky pieces.

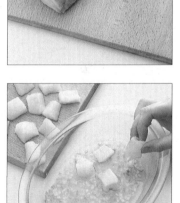

On 4 long or 8 short bamboo skewers, alternate fish with cubes of bell pepper, mango and banana. Arrange skewers in a broiler pan and spoon marinade over skewers. Broil 12 to 15 minutes, turning frequently and basting with marinade, or until cooked through. Serve with lime wedges.

Makes 4 servings.

Variation: Substitute fresh pineapple for mango.

SINGAPORE CURRY PUFFS

1 cup all-purpose flour
1 egg
⅔ cup milk
⅔ cup cold water
About 5 tablespoons corn oil
1 onion, chopped
8 ounces lean ground beef
2 carrots, grated
1 parsnip, grated
2 teaspoons Curry Powder, page 8
1 tablespoon tomato paste
2 teaspoons cornstarch
⅔ cup beef stock
1 egg, beaten
Vegetable oil for deep frying
Carrot strip, if desired

Sift flour into a bowl. Make a well in center and add egg. Gradually stir in milk and beat well until smooth. Stir in cold water and beat well. Pour batter into a pitcher.

Heat a little oil in a small skillet and pour off excess. Pour a little batter into skillet, swirling skillet to spread batter evenly over bottom to make a thin coating. Cook until underside is golden, then turn pancake out of pan (do not cook other side). Repeat with remaining batter, adding more oil to pan each time, to make 8 pancakes.

Heat 2 tablespoons oil in a saucepan. Add onion, ground beef, carrots, parsnip and curry powder. Cook gently 5 minutes, stirring constantly. Add tomato paste and mix well. Blend cornstarch with a little stock. Add remaining stock to ground beef mixture and bring to a boil. Add cornstarch mixture and cook 2 minutes, stirring constantly. Simmer mixture 10 minutes.

Lay pancakes, cooked-sides up, on a flat surface. Spread filling in a 2-inch-horizontal line across center to within 1-½ inches of side edges. Fold these side edges over mixture and then fold remaining top and bottom edges over to cover filling. Brush with egg and fold pancakes in half. Chill 1 hour.

Half fill a deep fat fryer or saucepan with oil; heat to 350F (175C) or until a ½-inch bread cube browns in 40 seconds. Fry folded pancakes, 4 at a time, 2 to 3 minutes or until golden brown and heated through. Drain on paper towels. Garnish with carrot strips, if desired, and serve hot.

Makes 8 servings.

DEVILED CRAB QUICHE

2 cups all-purpose flour
½ teaspoon salt
½ teaspoon chile seasoning
¼ cup cold margarine, diced
¼ cup lard, diced
½ cup (2 oz.) finely grated Cheddar cheese
3 tablespoons cold water
6 slices bacon, chopped
1 onion, chopped
4 ounces crabmeat, flaked
3 eggs
⅔ cup half and half
½ teaspoon mustard powder
¼ teaspoon cayenne pepper
Salt to taste
Tomato slices, if desired
Fresh Italian parsley sprigs, if desired

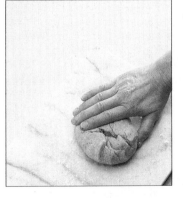

Preheat oven to 400F (205C). In a bowl, combine flour, salt and chile seasoning. Cut in margarine and lard until mixture resembles bread crumbs. Add cheese and mix well. Stir in cold water and mix to form a fairly firm dough. Knead gently on a floured surface and roll out pastry. Set a 10-inch fluted flan pan with a removable bottom on a baking sheet. Press pastry into flutes and trim edge neatly. Prick base with a fork. Line pastry with waxed paper and fill with dried beans.

Bake 15 minutes. Remove waxed paper and beans and bake 5 to 10 minutes more or until dry and lightly golden. Fry bacon 3 minutes. Add onion; cook 2 minutes. Remove from heat; mix with crabmeat. Spoon mixture into flan shell. Whisk eggs, half and half, mustard, cayenne and salt. Pour into flan shell. Bake 30 to 35 minutes or until set and lightly golden. Garnish with tomato and parsley, if desired, and serve warm or cold.

Makes 6 to 8 servings.

MUSTARD MOZZARELLA PORK

1 tablespoon butter
1 tablespoon oil
4 (6-oz.) pork steaks
1 onion, finely chopped
1 clove garlic, crushed
1 tablespoon Dijon-style mustard
¼ cup dry white wine
3 tablespoons half and half
Salt and freshly ground pepper to taste
1-¼ cups chopped Mozzarella cheese
Lemon wedges, if desired
Cucumber slices, if desired
Sliced celery, if desired
Fresh watercress sprigs, if desired

Heat butter and oil in a skillet. Add pork steaks and fry quickly 3 minutes on each side.

Cover and cook gently 15 minutes, turning occasionally. Remove pork steaks to a shallow flameproof dish; keep warm. Add onion and garlic to skillet and cook 5 minutes.

Add mustard and wine to onion mixture. Stir well, then bring to a boil. Boil 1-½ minutes. Stir in half and half and heat through gently. Season with salt and pepper. Spoon mixture over pork steaks and sprinkle with cheese. Preheat broiler. Broil 5 minutes or until cheese is melted and bubbling. Serve hot with lemon wedges, cucumber slices, celery and watercress sprigs, if desired.

Makes 4 servings.

CHILE BEAN TACOS

TANGY GLAZED DRUMSTICKS

2 tablespoons olive oil
1 pound pork sausage, crumbled
1 onion, chopped
1 clove garlic, crushed
½ teaspoon ground cumin
1 teaspoon hot chile powder
1 tomato, peeled, chopped
3 tablespoons tomato paste
½ red bell pepper, seeded, diced
1 (10-oz.) can kidney beans, drained
Salt to taste
8 taco shells
Sour cream
Paprika
Lettuce leaves
Raddish roses

Preheat oven to 350F (175C). Heat oil in a saucepan. Add sausage, onion, garlic, cumin and chile powder; fry gently 5 minutes, stirring to break up sausage. Add tomato, tomato paste, bell pepper and kidney beans. Stir well and cook gently 15 minutes, stirring frequently to prevent mixture sticking. Season with salt.

Meanwhile, heat taco shells following package instructions. Fill hot taco shells with sausage mixture. Top each taco with sour cream and sprinkle with paprika. Serve with lettuce leaves and radish roses.

Makes 8 tacos.

Variation: Substitute lean ground beef for sausage, if desired.

1 small onion, chopped
1 tablespoon honey
1 clove garlic, crushed
3 tablespoons corn oil
3 tablespoons catsup
1 tablespoon tomato paste
2 teaspoons Worcestershire sauce
1 teaspoon chile sauce
2 pinches Five Spice Powder, page 8
8 chicken drumsticks
Fresh watercress sprigs, if desired
Lemon slices, if desired

In a saucepan, combine onion, honey, garlic, 2 tablespoons of oil, catsup and tomato paste.

Add Worcestershire sauce, chile sauce and Five Spice Powder and simmer, uncovered, 5 minutes, stirring occasionally. In a blender or food processor, process mixture to a smooth purée. Add remaining oil and stir well.

Arrange chicken in a roasting pan. Brush with marinade and let stand 1 hour. Meanwhile, preheat oven to 400F (205C). Bake chicken in preheated oven 35 to 40 minutes, turning and brushing frequently with marinade juices. Serve hot or cold, garnished with watercress sprigs and lemon slices, if desired.

Makes 4 servings.

CLAM & SHRIMP CHOWDER

STIR-FRY PORK & PEPPERS

¼ cup butter
1 large onion, chopped
2 stalks celery, chopped
2 potatoes, peeled, diced
1-½ teaspoons fennel seeds
2 tablespoons all-purpose flour
1 teaspoon paprika
1-¾ cups chicken stock
1 (10-oz.) can baby clams, drained
4 ounces cooked peeled medium-size shrimp, thawed
   if frozen
1 red bell pepper, seeded, diced
¾ cup frozen corn, thawed
⅔ cup half and half
Salt and freshly ground pepper to taste
Fresh dill sprig, if desired

3 pinches Five Spice Powder, page 8
2 tablespoons dry sherry or sake
2 tablespoons light soy sauce
1 clove garlic, crushed
1 (1-inch) piece ginger root, peeled, chopped
1 pound pork tenderloin, cut in thin strips
2 onions
¼ cup corn oil
1 red bell pepper, seeded, cut in thin strips
1 green bell pepper, seeded, cut in thin strips
3 ounces button mushrooms, sliced
6 canned whole water chestnuts, sliced
2 teaspoons cornstarch
⅔ cup chicken stock
Leek curls, if desired
Green onion curls, if desired

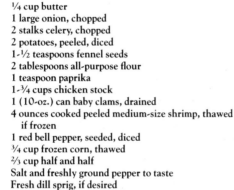

Melt butter in a saucepan. Add onion, celery, potatoes and fennel. Cook gently 5 minutes, stirring frequently. Blend in flour and cook 1 minute. Stir in paprika and stock and bring to a boil, stirring constantly.

In a bowl, combine Five Spice Powder, sherry, soy sauce, garlic and ginger. Add pork, stir well and let stand 30 minutes. Cut onions in eighths and separate in layers. Heat 2 tablespoons of oil in a skillet or wok. Drain pork, reserve marinade. Add pork to oil and stir-fry 5 minutes. Remove from skillet and keep warm.

Cover, reduce heat and simmer 15 minutes, stirring occasionally. Stir in clams, shrimp, bell pepper and corn. Simmer 5 minutes. Stir in half and half, salt and pepper. Garnish with dill sprig, if desired, and serve hot.

Makes 4 servings.

Variation: Omit paprika and add 1 teaspoon Curry Powder, page 8. Add 1 tablespoon chopped fresh parsley or cilantro just before serving.

Add remaining oil to skillet. Add onions, bell peppers, mushrooms and water chestnuts. Stir-fry 3 minutes. Add vegetable mixture to pork. Blend cornstarch with reserved marinade and 2 tablespoons of stock. Add remaining stock to skillet and bring to a boil. Add cornstarch mixture and cook 2 minutes, stirring constantly. Add pork and vegetables to stock and heat through, stirring constantly. Garnish with leek and green onion curls, if desired, and serve hot.

Makes 4 servings.

STEAK AU POIVRE

1-½ teaspoons green peppercorns
1 teaspoon black peppercorns
1 teaspoon white peppercorns
4 (6-oz.) boneless strip beef steaks
3 tablespoons unsalted butter
Few drops hot-pepper sauce
Few drops Worcestershire sauce
2 tablespoons brandy
3 tablespoons whipping cream
Salt to taste

Coarsely crush all peppercorns in a pestle and mortar.

Sprinkle crushed pepper over both sides of steaks, pressing in well with palm of hand. Let stand 30 minutes. Melt 1 tablespoon of butter in a skillet and heat until foaming. Add steaks and cook 2 to 3 minutes, then turn and cook other sides 2 to 3 minutes. (This timing gives medium-rare steaks, so adjust cooking time to suit personal preference.)

Turn steaks again and top each one with remaining butter and sprinkle with a few drops hot-pepper sauce and Worcestershire sauce. Pour brandy over steaks and allow to heat through a few seconds. Flame and remove from heat. When flames subside, remove steaks to a warm serving plate and keep warm. Add whipping cream to skillet and stir well. Heat through 1 minute, scraping up sediment from bottom of skillet. Season with salt and spoon mixture over steaks. Serve at once.

Makes 4 servings.

NOTE: Serve with fried potatoes and a green salad. Garnish with a fresh Italian parsley sprig, if desired.

CREOLE JAMBALAYA

2 tablespoons olive oil
8 ounces ham, diced
8 ounces chorizo sausage, sliced
1 large Spanish onion, chopped
3 cloves garlic, crushed
½ teaspoon dried thyme
2 tablespoons chopped fresh parsley
1-½ cups boiling chicken stock
1-½ cups long grain white rice
¼ teaspoon cayenne pepper
1 teaspoon hot-pepper sauce
1 (14-oz.) can tomatoes
1 green bell pepper, seeded, diced
2 tablespoons dry white wine
Tomato slices, if desired
Fresh thyme sprigs, if desired

Heat oil in a saucepan. Add ham, sausage and onion. Fry gently 3 minutes. Add garlic, thyme and parsley. Stir well, then add stock, rice, cayenne and hot-pepper sauce; mix well. Add tomatoes with juice and break up with a spoon. Bring mixture to a boil, stir well, then cover and simmer gently 15 minutes.

Stir in bell pepper and wine. Cover and cook 8 minutes or until liquid is absorbed. Fluff with a fork. Garnish with tomato slices and thyme sprigs, if desired, and serve hot.

Makes 4 to 6 servings.

Variation: Add 4 ounces cooked peeled medium-size shrimp, thawed, if frozen, to mixture 5 minutes before end of cooking time. For a fierier flavor, add more cayenne and hot-pepper sauce to taste.

VEGETABLE COUSCOUS

CHILE-CHEESE BURGERS

8 ounces couscous
2 cups water
¼ cup olive oil
2 onions, coarsely chopped
1 large eggplant, diced
1 (1-lb.) acorn squash, seeded, diced
2 carrots, sliced
1 teaspoon Harissa, page 8
2 tomatoes, peeled, chopped
2 tablespoons tomato paste
2 cups vegetable stock
1 (13-oz.) can garbanzo beans, drained
2 zucchini, sliced
⅓ cup raisins
2 tablespoons chopped fresh parsley
Fresh cilantro sprig, if desired

2 tablespoons olive oil
2 onions, finely chopped
2 cloves garlic, crushed
1 (8-oz.) can tomatoes in tomato juice
1 (3-½-oz.) can green chiles
1 tablespoon chile relish
½ teaspoon cumin seeds
1 pound lean ground beef
Salt and freshly ground pepper to taste
2 tablespoons corn oil
4 slices Gruyère cheese
Shredded lettuce
4 buns, split, warmed
Onion slices

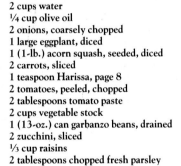

Combine couscous and water in a bowl. Let soak 15 minutes or until water is absorbed. Heat oil in a saucepan. Add onions, eggplant, squash and carrots and fry 5 minutes, stirring frequently. Stir in Harissa, tomatoes, tomato paste and stock. Bring to the boil and stir well.

Heat olive oil in a saucepan. Add 1 chopped onion and garlic and fry gently 5 minutes. Process tomatoes in a blender or food processor to a purée. Drain and chop chiles. Add tomatoes, chiles, chile relish and cumin to onion mixture. Stir well, then cover and simmer 10 minutes, stirring occasionally.

Line a large metal sieve or colander with muslin or all-purpose kitchen cloth and place over pan. Spoon couscous into sieve. Cover pan with foil to enclose steam and simmer 20 minutes. Remove sieve. Add garbanzo beans, zucchini and raisins to vegetable mixture. Stir well, then replace sieve and fluff couscous with a fork. Cover again with foil and simmer 20 minutes. Spoon couscous on a large serving dish and fluff with a fork. Add parsley to vegetable mixture and spoon over couscous. Garnish with cilantro sprig, if desired, and serve hot.

Makes 4 to 6 servings.

Meanwhile, put ground beef into a bowl. Add remaining onion, salt and pepper; mix well. Divide into 4 equal balls and shape each in a 4-½-inch round burger. Heat corn oil in a large skillet. Add burgers and fry 5 to 6 minutes on each side. Top each with a slice of cheese. Arrange lettuce on 4 bun halves. Place burger on lettuce and top with chile sauce, onion and remaining bun halves. Serve hot in napkins.

Makes 4 servings.

CHILE CON CARNE

2 tablespoons olive oil
1-½ pounds lean ground beef
2 onions, chopped
1 clove garlic, crushed
2 stalks celery, chopped
2 teaspoons hot chile powder
1 teaspoon cumin seeds
1 (14-oz.) can tomatoes
2 tablespoons tomato paste
1 (15-oz.) can red kidney beans, drained
Salt to taste
Steamed rice
Sour cream
Diced avocado
Onion slices
Fresh Italian parsley sprig, if desired

Preheat oven to 350F (175C). Heat oil in a flameproof casserole dish. Add ground beef, onions, garlic and celery and fry gently 5 minutes, stirring occasionally.

Add chile powder and cumin and cook gently 2 minutes. Add tomatoes and break up with a spoon. Stir in tomato paste and kidney beans. Bring to a boil, stirring frequently.

Cover and bake in preheated oven 1 hour, stirring occasionally. Season mixture with salt. Spoon chile over individual bowls of rice and top each serving with sour cream, avocado and onion. Garnish with parsley sprig, if desired.

Makes 4 servings.

NOTE: For a fierier flavor, increase chile powder to 1 tablespoon. To prevent avocado discoloring, toss in lemon juice.

NASI GORENG

1-½ cups long grain white rice
3 tablespoons corn oil
2 onions, cut in half, sliced
2 cloves garlic, crushed
2 small fresh green chiles, seeded, chopped
1 (6-oz.) pork tenderloin, diced
1 (6-oz.) skinned chicken breast
¼ teaspoon hot chile powder
1 teaspoon paprika
2 tablespoons light soy sauce
4 ounces cooked peeled medium-size shrimp, thawed
    if frozen
Salt to taste
1 egg
1 teaspoon cold water
1-½ teaspoons butter
Shrimp crackers

Cook rice in boiling, salted water 12 minutes. Drain and rinse well, then drain again. Heat oil in a large skillet. Add onions, garlic and chiles and fry 2 minutes. Add pork and chicken and fry gently 10 minutes until cooked. Add rice, chile powder, paprika, soy sauce and shrimp and cook 5 to 6 minutes or until piping hot, stirring constantly. Season with salt.

Turn mixture into a warm serving dish and keep warm while preparing omelette topping. Whisk egg with cold water. Melt butter in a skillet. Add egg mixture and swirl skillet over gentle heat 2 to 3 minutes or until egg mixture is set and lightly golden underneath. Turn omelette out onto a flat surface. Roll up and cut in slices. Arrange slices of omelette on top of rice mixture. Serve hot with shrimp crackers.

Makes 4 servings.

INDONESIAN COCONUT BEEF

CHILE PEPPER PIZZA

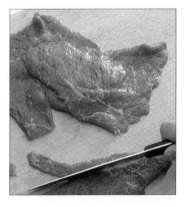

1-½ pounds boneless sirloin steak, trimmed
3 tablespoons corn oil
1 large Spanish onion, sliced
1 clove garlic, crushed
1 teaspoon ground ginger
1 teaspoon ground cumin
1 teaspoon ground coriander
1 teaspoon chile seasoning
⅔ cup shredded coconut
2 teaspoons light-brown sugar
1 tablespoon lemon juice
1-¼ cups beef stock
Thin slivers red bell pepper
Chopped green chiles
Small slices onion

3 tablespoons olive oil
1 onion, cut in fourths, sliced
1 clove garlic, crushed
1 (8-oz.) can tomatoes
1 tablespoon tomato paste
½ teaspoon dried oregano
1 cup all-purpose flour
1 cup whole-wheat flour
¼ teaspoon salt
1 teaspoon active dried yeast
⅔ cup warm water (120F-130F/50C-55C)
1 (3-½-oz.) can green chiles
6 ounces Mozzarella cheese, chopped
2 ounces pepperoni or salami stick, sliced
8 ripe or green olives
Tomato roses, if desired
Fresh parsley sprigs, if desired

Cut steak in ½-inch thick strips.

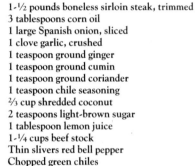

Heat oil in a saucepan. Add Spanish onion slices and garlic and fry gently until soft. Add beef and fry, stirring, until brown.

Lightly grease a 10-inch pizza pan. Heat 2 tablespoons of oil in a saucepan. Add onion, garlic, tomato paste, tomatoes with juice and oregano. Stir well to break up tomatoes, then simmer, uncovered, 10 to 15 minutes or until well thickened; cool. Preheat oven to 375F (190C). Put flours, salt and yeast in a bowl and mix well. Add water and mix to form a dough. Knead well, then roll to a 10-inch circle. Line greased pizza pan with dough.

Add spices to beef and cook 2 minutes. Add coconut, brown sugar, lemon juice and beef stock; stir well. Simmer gently, uncovered, 30 to 35 minutes, stirring occasionally, or until mixture is thickened and dry. Stir mixture more frequently towards end of cooking time to prevent sticking. Garnish with slivers of bell pepper, green chiles and small slices onion.

Brush surface of dough with a little of remaining oil and cover with tomato mixture. Drain and chop chiles and sprinkle on top. Sprinkle with cheese and drizzle with remaining oil. Bake in preheated oven 25 minutes. Top pizza with pepperoni or salami and olives and bake 10 minutes. Cut in wedges. Garnish with tomato roses and parsley sprigs, if desired, and serve hot.

Makes 4 servings.

Makes 2 to 4 servings.

NOTE: If you prefer a more moist mixture, cook 20 to 25 minutes instead of 30 to 35 minutes.

VEGETARIAN LENTIL MEDLEY

⅔ cup whole green lentils
⅔ cup split peas
2-½ cups cold water
2 leeks, cut into ¼-inch slices
2 zucchini, cut into ¼-inch slices
2 carrots, thinly sliced
2 stalks celery, thinly sliced
1 onion, coarsely chopped
1 clove garlic, crushed
2 tablespoons ghee
½ teaspoon turmeric
1 teaspoon mustard seeds
2 teaspoons Garam Masala, page 8
Salt to taste
Fresh celery leaves
Lemon slices

Soak lentils and peas overnight. Drain lentils and peas and put into a saucepan. Add cold water, bring to a boil and boil 10 minutes. Add vegetables and garlic, cover and cook gently 10 minutes.

Meanwhile, melt ghee in a saucepan. Add turmeric, mustard seeds and Garam Masala and cook gently 2 minutes or until seeds begin to pop. Stir into lentil mixture and cook 15 minutes or until vegetables and lentils are tender and liquid has been absorbed. Season with salt. Garnish with celery leaves and lemon slices and serve hot.

Makes 4 servings.

CHEESY SPANISH OMELET

1 tablespoon olive oil
2 tablespons butter
1 onion, chopped
1 clove garlic, crushed
1 red bell pepper, seeded, diced
¾ cup finely shredded green cabbage
4 slices bacon, chopped
1 teaspoon fenugreek
½ teaspoon ground coriander
4 eggs, beaten
1 tablespoon cold water
Salt and freshly ground pepper to taste
½ cup (1-½ oz.) grated Cheddar cheese
Red bell pepper strips, if desired
Fresh Italian parsley sprigs, if desired

Heat oil and butter in a medium-size flame-proof skillet. Add onion, garlic, bell pepper, cabbage and bacon and fry over low heat 5 minutes, stirring occasionally. Add fenugreek and coriander and stir well.

Preheat broiler. Whisk eggs with cold water, salt and pepper and pour into skillet. Swirl skillet to ensure an even coating. Cook over low heat 3 to 4 minutes or until mixture is golden brown underneath. Sprinkle with cheese and place under preheated broiler and cook until mixture is set on top and cheese has melted. Cut in 4 wedges, garnish with bell pepper strips and parsley sprigs, if desired, and serve hot.

Makes 4 servings.

FALAFEL

1 (13-oz.) can garbanzo beans, drained
1 onion, cut in fourths
2 cloves garlic
4 slices fresh white bread, cubed
¼ teaspoon cumin seeds
4 small dried red chiles, crushed
1 tablespoon chopped fresh parsley
Salt and freshly ground pepper to taste
1 egg, beaten
⅓ cup dry fine bread crumbs
Vegetable oil for deep frying
4 pieces pita bread, warmed
Shredded lettuce
Onion slices
Tomato slices

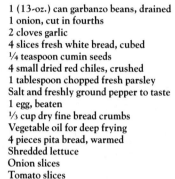

Process garbanzo beans, onion, garlic, bread, cumin and chiles in a blender or food processor until smooth, then spoon mixture into a bowl. Add parsley, salt, pepper and egg; mix well. Form in 8 balls and coat in bread crumbs. Flatten balls slightly to form oval shapes.

Half fill a deep fat fryer or saucepan with oil; heat to 375F (190C) or until a ½-inch cube of day-old bread browns in 40 seconds. Fry Falafel, a few at a time, 3 minutes or until golden brown. Drain on paper towels. Cut pita bread in half and open to form pockets. Put 1 Falafel into each pocket with lettuce, onion and tomato slices and serve hot.

Makes 8 servings.

CEYLONESE CHICKEN CURRY

2 large onions
1 (2-inch) piece ginger root, peeled, chopped
2 cloves garlic, peeled
2 tablespoons water
5 tablespoons corn oil
2-½ to 3 tablespoons Curry Powder, page 8
1-½ pounds boneless chicken breasts, skinned
1-½ tablespoons all-purpose flour
1-½ cups chicken stock
2 stalks celery, sliced
1 red or green bell pepper, seeded, diced
½ teaspoon cumin seeds
3 ounces button mushrooms, if desired
¾ ounce creamed coconut, chopped
2 tomatoes, peeled, seeded, sliced
Toasted shredded coconut
Fresh chervil sprigs, if desired

Cut 1 onion in fourths. In a blender or food processor, process onion, ginger and garlic until very finely chopped. Heat 3 tablespoons of oil in a saucepan. Add onion mixture and Curry Powder and fry 2 minutes, stirring constantly. Cut chicken in bite-size cubes and add to onion mixture. Fry until chicken is seared. Stir in flour and cook 1 minute. Stir in stock and bring to a boil. Cover and simmer gently 15 minutes.

Meanwhile, peel remaining onion and separate in rings. Heat remaining oil in a skillet. Add celery, onion rings, bell pepper, cumin seeds and mushrooms, if desired, and fry gently 4 minutes. Add vegetable mixture to chicken mixture and cook 15 minutes. Stir in creamed coconut. Add tomatoes and heat through. Garnish with shredded coconut and chervil sprigs, if desired, and serve hot.

Makes 6 to 8 servings.

BARBECUE SAUCE

3 tablespoons corn oil
1 small onion, finely chopped
1 clove garlic, crushed
½ teaspoon dry mustard
2 tablespoons malt vinegar
1 tablespoon Worcestershire sauce
2 tablespoons light-brown sugar
3 tablespoons catsup
½ teaspoon chile seasoning
¾ cup chicken stock
Fresh Italian parsley sprig, if desired

Heat oil in a small saucepan. Add onion and garlic and cook gently 2 minutes, stirring frequently.

Stir in mustard, vinegar, Worcestershire sauce, sugar, catsup, chile seasoning and stock. Bring to a boil.

Cover and simmer sauce gently 7 to 8 minutes or until slightly thickened. Garnish with parsley sprig, if desired.

Makes 1-¼ cups.

NOTE: Serve hot as a sauce with hamburgers, hot dogs or fried chicken. Or, if preferred, allow to cool and use to brush over meats, poultry and fish while baking or grilling.

WINE & PEPPER CREAM SAUCE

2 tablespoons unsalted butter
2 shallots, finely chopped
1 tablespoon brandy
½ cup dry white wine
½ cup chicken stock
2 teaspoons green peppercorns, coarsely crushed
3 tablespoons whipping cream
1 tablespoon chopped fresh parsley
Fresh parsley sprig, if desired

Melt butter in a skillet. Add shallots and cook gently 3 minutes. Add brandy to pan and allow to heat through a few seconds, then flame. When flames subside, add wine to shallots.

Stir in stock and peppercorns and boil rapidly 2 to 3 minutes or until slightly reduced.

Remove from heat and stir in cream and chopped parsley. Return to medium heat and heat through 2 to 3 minutes, stirring constantly. Garnish with parsley sprig, if desired.

Makes ¾ cup.

NOTE: Serve hot with steaks, veal or fish dishes.

TANGY MUSTARD SAUCE

SWEET SPICY CHILE SAUCE

3 tablespoons butter
1 small onion, finely chopped
¼ cup all-purpose flour
1 cup chicken stock
⅔ cup milk
1 bay leaf
1 teaspoon coarsely ground mustard
2 teaspoons dry mustard
1 tablespoon wine vinegar
1 teaspoon sugar
Salt and freshly ground pepper to taste
Additional fresh bay leaves, if desired

Melt butter in a saucepan. Add onion and cook gently 2 minutes. Stir in flour and cook 1 minute.

Stir in stock and bring to a boil, stirring constantly. Reduce heat and simmer 2 minutes, stirring constantly. Add milk and bay leaf, stir well and cook 2 minutes.

Blend mustards smoothly with vinegar and sugar. Add mustard mixture, salt and pepper to stock mixture and heat through 2 to 3 minutes. Remove bay leaf. Garnish with fresh bay leaves, if desired.

Makes 1-¾ cups.

NOTE: This recipe makes a thick sauce. If a thinner sauce is desired, add a little more stock or milk. Serve sauce hot with smoked sausage, rabbit and fish dishes.

1 clove garlic
1 Spanish onion, cut in fourths
2 fresh green chiles, seeded
2 tablespoons corn oil
½ teaspoon ground ginger
1 (8-oz.) can tomatoes in tomato juice
⅓ cup seedless raisins
1 tablespoon lemon juice
1 tablespoon dark soy sauce
2 tablespoons light-brown sugar
Salt and freshly ground pepper to taste
Fresh parsley sprig, if desired

In a blender or food processor, finely chop garlic, onion and chiles.

Heat oil in a saucepan. Add onion mixture and ginger and cook gently 3 minutes. Add tomatoes and break up with a spoon. Stir in raisins, lemon juice, soy sauce, brown sugar and water.

Bring to a boil, reduce heat and simmer 15 minutes, uncovered. Process in a blender or food processor to desired consistency. Reheat and season with salt and pepper. Garnish with parsley sprig, if desired.

Makes 2-½ cups.

NOTE: Serve hot with grilled steak, fried chicken or grilled whitefish.

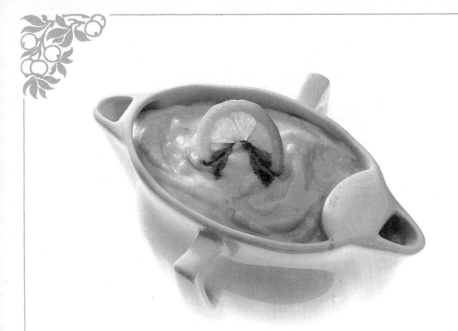

LEMON BUTTER HOLLANDAISE

¼ cup lemon juice
1 teaspoon black peppercorns
3 blades mace
2 large egg yolks
½ cup butter, room temperature
3 good pinches cayenne pepper
Lemon slice, if desired
Paprika

Put lemon juice, peppercorns and mace into a small saucepan. Bring to a boil and boil until liquid is reduced by half. In a bowl, combine egg yolks with 1 tablespoon of butter and beat well.

Strain hot lemon liquid into butter mixture, beating constantly with a wooden spoon. Place pan over a very low heat and gradually add small pieces of remaining butter, whisking well until sauce is thickened and smooth. (If mixture gets too hot at this stage it will curdle and separate. To prevent this from happening, keep removing pan from heat while beating in butter to ensure gentle cooking).

Add cayenne pepper to sauce and mix well. Turn mixture into a warm serving dish. Garnish with lemon slice, if desired, and sprinkle with paprika.

Makes ⅔ cup.

NOTE: This rich egg and butter sauce requires great care during cooking to achieve delicious results. Serve warm or cold with poached salmon, asparagus or globe artichokes.

INDONESIAN COCONUT SAUCE

1 cup shredded coconut
1-⅔ cups boiling water
3 tablespoons corn oil
1 onion, cut in fourths, then in thin slices
1 clove garlic, crushed
1 tablespoon Curry Powder, page 8
½ teaspoon turmeric
½ teaspoon ground cilantro
½ teaspoon hot chile powder
1 tablespoon cornstarch
1 tablespoon lemon juice
1 large tomato, peeled, seeded
½ small green bell pepper, seeded
Salt to taste

In a blender or food processor, process coconut and boiling water 45 seconds. Strain mixture through a fine sieve, pressing coconut firmly to extract all liquid. Heat oil in a saucepan. Add onion, garlic, Curry Powder, turmeric, coriander and chile powder and fry gently 3 minutes, stirring.

Add coconut milk and bring to a boil. Cover and simmer gently 5 minutes. Blend cornstarch and lemon juice until smooth and add to coconut mixture. Bring to a boil and cook 2 minutes, stirring constantly. Cut tomato and bell pepper in thin slivers and add to sauce. Cook gently 5 minutes. Season with salt.

Makes 2-¼ cups.

NOTE: Serve hot with grilled steak and chicken or stir-fry dishes.

ROAST PEPPER RELISH

PIQUANT ORIENTAL SAUCE

1 yellow bell pepper, seeded, cut in half
1 red bell pepper, seeded, cut in half
1 green bell pepper, seeded, cut in half
1 onion, cut in fourths, then in thin slices
1/3 cup corn oil
2 tablespoons lemon juice
1 teaspoon coarsely ground mustard
1 clove garlic, crushed
1/2 teaspoon Garam Masala, page 8
1-1/2 teaspoons sugar
Salt and freshly ground pepper to taste

Preheat oven to 400F (205C). Place peppers, cut-sides down, in a roasting pan.

Bake in preheated oven 30 minutes or until skins begin to blister and blacken. Cool peppers, then peel. Cut peppers in fourths and slice in thin strips. Put peppers into a shallow dish. Sprinkle with onion.

Combine remaining ingredients in a screw-topped jar and shake vigorously until well blended. Pour mixture over peppers and marinate several hours, stirring occasionally.

Makes 4 servings.

NOTE: Store in refrigerator up to 3 days. Garnish with a fresh cilantro sprig, if desired and serve chilled as an accompaniment to game pies, cold meats or crusty bread and cheese.

2 tablespoons corn oil
1 onion, cut in fourths, then in thin slices
1 carrot, cut in julienne strips
1/2 green bell pepper, seeded, cut in thin strips
1 (1-1/2-inch) piece ginger root, peeled, chopped
3 good pinches Five Spice Powder, page 8
1 (8-oz.) can pineapple slices
1 tablespoon sugar
1 tablespoon dark soy sauce
1 tablespoon dry sherry
1 tablespoon malt vinegar
1-1/2 tablespoons catsup
1 tablespoon cornstarch
2/3 cup chicken stock
Fresh pineapple leaves, if desired

Heat oil in a saucepan. Add onion, carrot, bell pepper and ginger and stir-fry 3 minutes. Add Five Spice Powder and remove from heat. Drain pineapple slices, reserving juice. Add enough water to make 2/3 cup liquid. Cut 2 pineapple slices in thin pieces; reserve remaining pineapple slices for another use.

In a bowl, mix together sugar, soy sauce, sherry, vinegar, catsup and pineapple juice. Add pineapple juice mixture and pineapple pieces to vegetables. Blend cornstarch smoothly with a little stock, then add remaining stock. Add stock to vegetable mixture and bring to a boil, stirring constantly. Reduce heat and simmer 2 minutes, stirring constantly. Garnish with pineapple leaves, if desired.

Makes 2-1/2 cups.

NOTE: Serve hot with fried chicken, pork steaks or shellfish.

PICCALILLI

4 ounces French green beans, ends removed, cut in
   1-inch pieces
8 ounces cauliflower flowerets
8 ounces small pickling onions, peeled
1 (8-oz.) piece cucumber, diced
½ cup pickling salt
1 teaspoon turmeric
1 tablespoon dry mustard
½ teaspoon ground ginger
⅓ cup sugar
1-¾ cups distilled malt vinegar
4 teaspoons cornstarch

Layer all vegetables in a colander with salt.
Let stand overnight.

Wash 3 pint jars in hot soapy water; rinse.
Keep hot until needed. Prepare lids as
manufacturer directs. Rinse vegetables well
under cold running water and drain
thoroughly. Mix turmeric, mustard, ginger
and sugar with 1-½ cups vinegar and blend
well. Pour mixture into a saucepan and add
vegetables. Simmer gently 9 to 10 minutes
or until vegetables are crisp-tender.

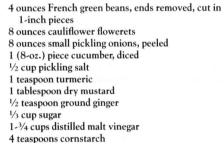

Blend cornstarch to a smooth paste with
remaining vinegar. Add to vegetable mixture and mix well. Bring to a boil and cook 3
minutes, stirring carefully to prevent
damaging vegetables. Ladle hot relish into 1
hot jar at a time, leaving ¼-inch head-
space. Release trapped air. Wipe rim of jar
with a clean damp cloth. Attach lid and
place in canner. Fill and close remaining
jars. Process 10 minutes in a boiling-water
bath.

Makes about 3 pints.

NOTE: Garnish with cucumber slices, if
desired, and serve with cold pies, salads and
sandwiches.

YOGURT TOMATO COOLER

1 tablespoon corn oil
2 cloves garlic, crushed
½ teaspoon cumin seeds
1 cup plain yogurt
½ teaspoon paprika
2 firm tomatoes, finely chopped
4 green onions, finely chopped
2 tablespoons chopped fresh mint
Salt and freshly ground pepper to taste
Fresh mint sprigs

Heat oil in a small saucepan. Add garlic and
cumin seeds and cook very gently 2 minutes.
Remove from heat and cool.

In a bowl, combine cooled garlic mixture,
yogurt, paprika and stir well. Add tomatoes,
green onions, chopped mint, salt and
pepper.

Spoon mixture into a serving bowl and chill
several hours. Garnish with mint sprigs.

Makes 4 servings.

Variation: Omit tomatoes and onions and
add 1 peeled seeded finely chopped or grated
cucumber.

NOTE: Serve as an accompaniment to
curries or as a tasty sauce with hot buttered
Nan or pita bread.

PICKLED RED CABBAGE

1 (2-lb.) red cabbage
3 tablespoons pickling salt
2 tablespoons Pickling Spice, page 8
5 cups distilled malt vinegar
2 teaspoons caraway seeds

Cut cabbage in fourths and discard center stalk. Shred cabbage finely. Layer in a colander with salt and let stand overnight.

Put Pickling Spice and vinegar into a saucepan. Bring to a boil and boil 3 minutes. Remove from heat and cool. When cool, strain and reserve liquid. Meanwhile, wash 4 pint jars in hot soapy water; rinse. Keep hot until needed. Prepare lids as manufacturer directs.

Rinse cabbage well under cold running water. Drain thoroughly and mix with caraway seeds. Pack cabbage into hot jars. Pour cold spiced vinegar over cabbage to cover completely. Wipe rims of jars with a clean damp cloth. Attach lids and place in canner. Process 10 minutes in a boiling water bath. Store in a cool dry dark place at least 5 days before serving.

Makes about 4 pint jars.

NOTE: Use cabbage within 2 months; if left longer cabbage loses its crispness. Garnish with an Italian parsley sprig, if desired, and serve as an accompaniment to cold meats and poultry.

PEPPERED SALAMI SALAD

½ cup olive oil
2 cloves garlic, crushed
3 slices white bread, crusts removed, cubed
½ teaspoon chile seasoning
8 ounces young spinach or 1 cos lettuce
1 (6-oz.) piece peppered salami, diced
3 small onions, sliced, separated in rings
1 red bell pepper, seeded, cut in thin strips
4 ounces button mushrooms, sliced
1-½ tablespoons lemon juice
1 teaspoon sugar
1 teaspoon prepared mustard
Salt and freshly ground pepper to taste
12 olives

Heat 3 tablespoons of oil in a skillet. Add garlic and bread cubes and fry, stirring constantly, until golden. Remove from heat. Add chile seasoning, stir well and cool. Tear spinach or lettuce leaves in bite-size pieces. In a large salad bowl, combine spinach or lettuce leaves, salami, onion, bell pepper and mushrooms.

Place remaining oil in a screw-top jar with lemon juice, sugar, mustard, salt and pepper. Shake vigorously until well blended. Pour over salad and toss well. Sprinkle croutons on top and garnish with olives. Serve at once.

Makes 4 servings.

NOTE: Salad (without dressing) may be prepared in advance and kept covered in refrigerator. Just before serving, shake dressing ingredients vigorously, add to salad and toss well. Add croutons and olives and serve at once.

WINE GLAZED ORANGES

½ cup sugar
¾ cup water
¾ cup red wine
4 whole cloves
2 teaspoons cassia bark, broken in small pieces
1 small piece dried ginger root
4 large oranges
Grated orange peel, if desired
Half and half

In a saucepan, combine sugar and water and heat slowly, stirring to dissolve sugar. Add wine, cloves, cassia bark and ginger. Bring to a boil and boil until slightly thickened and syrupy. Cool 5 minutes.

Meanwhile, using a sharp knife, peel oranges, removing all bitter white pith. Cut oranges in ¼-inch-thick slices and place in a shallow dish. Strain wine syrup over oranges. Cover and chill several hours or overnight, turning slices occasionally in syrup.

Using wooden picks, secure orange slices together to form whole oranges and place in a serving dish. Pour wine syrup over oranges. Garnish with orange peel, if desired, and serve with half and half.

Makes 4 servings.

NOTE: If desired, serve oranges in slices rather than as whole oranges.

PEARS IN PINEAPPLE CREAM

1 tablespoon lemon juice
4 large firm pears
4 pieces crystallized ginger, cut in halves
2 tablespoons butter
1 tablespoon light-brown sugar
⅔ cup pineappple juice
⅔ cup whipping cream
Fresh bay leaves
Toasted flaked almonds

Preheat oven to 375F (190C). Lightly grease a shallow baking dish. Fill a bowl with cold water and add lemon juice. Peel pears and cut in half. Cut away stems and remove cores with a teaspoon. Drop prepared pears in lemon water.

Pat pears dry on paper towels. Place a piece of crystallized ginger into "well" of each pear half. Arrange, pears, cut-sides down, in greased dish.

Put butter, brown sugar and pineapple juice into a saucepan and heat gently to dissolve sugar. Add whippping cream and boil 5 minutes. Pour sauce over pears. Cover and bake in preheated oven 1 hour or until pears are tender and sauce has thickened. Baste pears with sauce several times during baking. Place pears on a warm serving plate and spoon sauce over pears. Arrange bay leaves to resemble pear leaves and garnish with almonds. Serve hot.

Makes 4 servings.

MELON & GINGER BASKET

LEMON GINGER SYLLABUBS

1 large ripe honeydew melon
¼ cup orange juice
1 to 2 pieces stem ginger, thinly sliced
2 tablespoons stem ginger syrup
Freshly grated nutmeg to taste
2 kiwifruit, peeled, cut in half, sliced
8 lychees, peeled, seeded
8 strawberries, cut in half
8 black grapes, cut in half, seeded
Fresh mint sprig, if desired
Ice cream

Cut a thin slice off one of the rounded sides of melon (not pointed ends), so melon will sit level on a serving plate.

To form a handle, make 2 cuts about ¾-inch wide on either side of a central strip. Continue cutting halfway down melon, then cut from bottom of handle around either side of fruit so these two wedges can be lifted away to form a basket shape. Cut away flesh from inside handle. Remove seeds from melon. Scoop out balls with a small melon scoop or cut flesh in pieces and place in a bowl. Smooth edge of melon basket.

Add orange juice, stem ginger and syrup and nutmeg to melon balls and stir lightly. Add kiwifruit, lychees, strawberries and grapes and mix lightly. Spoon mixture into melon and arrange fruits attractively. Cover and chill. Garnish with mint sprig, if desired, and serve with ice cream.

Makes 4 to 6 servings.

Variation: Use fresh fruits such as cherries, pineapple, peaches, figs and nectarines. Substitute freshly squeezed lime juice for orange juice.

1-¼ cups whipping cream
⅓ cup sugar
Finely grated peel 1 lemon
2 tablespoons lemon juice
2 pieces stem ginger, chopped
1 egg white
2 kiwifruit, peeled, cut in fourths, then sliced
4 teaspoons stem ginger syrup
Lemon twists
Stem ginger slices
Cookies

Whip cream and sugar until cream begins to thicken. Add lemon peel and juice and whisk until thick and velvety.

Fold in stem ginger. Whisk egg white stiffly and fold into cream mixture. Place kiwifruit in bottom of 4 glasses. Sprinkle with stem ginger syrup. Top with cream mixture and chill 2 hours.

Garnish with lemon and stem ginger. Serve with cookies.

Makes 4 servings.

Variation: Substitute pitted cherries, sliced peaches or nectarines for kiwifruit.

BERRIES WITH PEPPER SAUCE

1 lemon
1 cup sugar
²/₃ cup water
1-¼ cups orange juice
1 tablespoon green peppercorns, coarsely crushed
1 pound strawberries
Fresh mint leaves, if desired
Half and half, if desired

Finely grate peel from lemon and put into a saucepan. Squeeze juice from lemon and reserve. Add sugar and water to lemon peel and heat gently, stirring until sugar dissolves.

Bring to a boil and boil until syrup turns a light caramel color. Remove from heat and hold pan handle with a cloth as mixture will splatter. Stir in lemon and orange juices. Heat gently, stirring to dissolve caramel.

Stir in peppercorns and boil 3 to 4 minutes or until slightly thickened and syrupy. Allow to cool 2 minutes, then spoon hot syrup over strawberries. Garnish with mint, if desired, and serve at once with half and half, if desired.

Makes 4 servings.

GLAZED APPLE TART

1-½ cups all-purpose flour
Pinch salt
½ cup butter
3 tablespoons sugar
1 egg yolk
2 teaspoons cold water
4 Granny Smith apples
Finely grated peel ½ lemon
½ teaspoon cornstarch
½ teaspoon ground cinnamon
2 pinches ground nutmeg
5 tablespoons apricot jam
2 tablespoons lemon juice
Whipped cream
Fresh mint sprigs, if desired

Preheat oven to 375F (190C). Butter an 8-inch-round baking pan. To make pastry, sift flour and salt into a bowl. Add butter and cut in finely until mixture resembles bread crumbs. Stir in 1 tablespoon of sugar, egg yolk and cold water.

Knead gently until smooth and chill 15 minutes. Sprinkle with remaining sugar. Peel, core and cut apples in fairly thin slices. Arrange a layer of apple slices in overlapping circles in bottom of pan.

Mix remaining apple slices with lemon peel, cornstarch and spices. Spoon on top of arranged apple slices. Roll out pastry to an 8-inch circle. Place on top of apples and press gently. Prick several times with a fork. Bake in preheated oven 40 minutes or until pastry is golden brown. Carefully turn out tart onto a warm serving plate. Combine jam and lemon juice in a saucepan and heat gently until melted, stirring until smooth. Spoon hot jam mixture over tart. Serve hot or cold with whipped cream. Garnish with mint sprig, if desired.

Makes 6 to 8 servings.

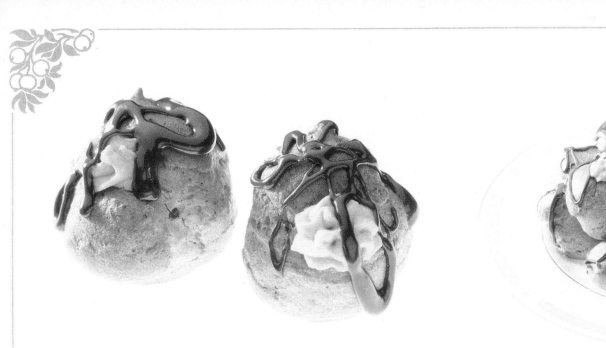

CHOC 'N' SPICE PROFITEROLES

½ cup plus 2 tablespoons all-purpose flour
1 teaspoon ground cinnamon
⅔ cup water
¼ cup plus 1-½ teaspoons butter, diced
2 eggs, beaten
1-¼ cups whipping cream
1 tablespoon powdered sugar
2 teaspoons coffee flavoring
4 ounces semisweet chocolate, broken in pieces
2 tablespoons Tia Maria
2 tablespoons light corn syrup
2 teaspoons superfine sugar

Preheat oven to 400F (205C). Lightly grease several baking sheets.

Sift flour and ½ teaspoon of cinnamon onto waxed paper. Pour water into a saucepan. Add 3-½ tablespoons butter and heat gently until butter melts. Do not allow water to boil before butter melts. Rapidly bring to boil, remove from heat and add flour all at once. Using a wooden spoon, stir quickly to form a smooth mixture. Return pan to medium heat a few seconds and beat well until dough forms a smooth ball and leaves sides of pan clean.

Remove from heat and cool slightly. Gradually add eggs, a little at a time, beating well after each addition to form a smooth shiny dough. Transfer dough to a pastry bag fitted with a ¾-inch plain tube. Pipe 24 small balls onto greased baking sheets.

Bake in preheated oven 20 minutes, then reduce oven temperature to 350F (175C) and continue cooking 15 to 20 minutes longer or until well risen, crisp and sound hollow when tapped on bottoms. Make a slit in side of each pastry to allow steam to escape. Cool on a wire rack.

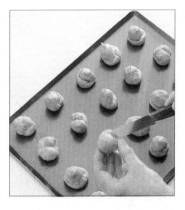

Whip cream, powdered sugar and coffee flavoring until thick. Spoon into a pastry bag fitted with a small star tube. Pipe cream into pastry or use a teaspoon to fill pastry with cream. Arrange profiteroles in a pyramid-shape on a serving dish.

Melt chocolate and remaining butter in a heatproof bowl set over a pan of gently simmering water. Stir in Tia Maria and corn syrup and continue stirring until sauce is smooth and coats back of a spoon. Spoon chocolate sauce over profiteroles and let stand a few minutes. Mix remaining ½ teaspoon of cinnamon with superfine sugar and sprinkle over profiteroles.

Makes 6 servings.

NOTE: Profiteroles are at their best seved 2 hours after assembling when they have softened slightly.

BAKLAVA

¼ cup sugar
1-⅓ cups blanched chopped almonds
¾ cup chopped walnuts
1-½ teaspoons ground cinnamon
½ teaspoon Mixed Spice, page 8
1 pound filo pastry
1 cup unsalted butter, melted
1-½ cups sugar
1-⅓ cups water
4 large pieces cassia bark
6 whole cloves
Lemon peel strip
2 tablespoons honey

In a bowl, combine ¼ cup sugar, almonds, walnuts, cinnamon and Mixed Spice.

Preheat oven to 325F (165C). Grease a 13″ × 9″ baking pan. Line bottom of pan with a sheet of filo pastry, trimming it to fit. Brush with melted butter and add another 7 sheets of filo, trimming and brushing each one with butter before adding next sheet. Sprinkle half of nut mixture over filo, then cover with 4 sheets of filo, trimming and brushing each one with melted butter. Sprinkle remaining nut mixture on top and cover with 5 more sheets of filo, trimming and brushing each one with melted butter. Spread any remaining butter on top.

Using a sharp knife, cut through top layers of pastry, first one way, then the other, to make 25 diamond-shaped pieces. Bake in preheated oven 1 hour or until golden brown. If necessary, cover with foil during cooking to prevent overbrowning. Cool in pan. Combine 1-½ cups sugar and water in a large saucepan. Add cassia bark, cloves, lemon peel and honey and heat gently, stirring to dissolve sugar. Boil 5 minutes, then strain warm syrup over filo and let stand overnight. *Makes about 25 pieces.*

CORNISH SAFFRON CAKE

3 (0.05 gram) packets saffron strands
1 tablespoon boiling water
⅓ cup sugar
1 cup warm water (110F/44C)
1 (¼-oz.) package active dried yeast
(about 1 tablespoon)
5 cups bread flour
¼ teaspoon salt
¾ cup lard
½ cup butter
1-⅔ cups currants or mixed fruit

Lightly grease 2 (9″ × 5″) loaf pans. Line a broiler pan with foil. Place saffron on foil and spread thinly. Place pan under a very low broiler and gently dry saffron (do not discolor) 3 to 4 minutes or until dry.

Place saffron in a small bowl and crush to a fine powder. Add boiling water and let stand 8 hours. Dissolve 1 teaspoon of sugar in ¼ cup warm water. Add yeast, whisk and let stand 10 to 15 minutes or until frothy. Put flour, salt, lard and butter into a bowl and cut fats in finely. Mix in remaining sugar and currants. Stir saffron into remaining warm water and add to flour mixture. Stir in yeast and mix to form a dough. Knead lightly, cover and let rise in a warm place until double in bulk.

Knead dough and divide in half. Press each piece to a rectangle with width equal to length of loaf pan. Roll up dough, jelly-roll style, and place in greased loaf pans, seam side down. Press to fill corners. Cover and let stand at room temperature until dough has risen to top of pans. Preheat oven to 375F (190C). Bake in preheated oven 35 to 45 minutes or until golden. If necessary, cover with foil during baking to prevent overbrowning. Cool on a wire rack. Let stand 1 day before serving. *Makes 2 cakes.*

FROSTED GINGERBREAD

2 cups all-purpose flour
¼ teaspoon salt
½ teaspoon Mixed Spice, page 8
1-½ teaspoons ground ginger
1 teaspoon baking soda
¼ cup light corn syrup
¼ cup molasses
⅓ cup hard margarine
½ cup dark-brown sugar
2 eggs, beaten
1 cup milk
1 (3-oz.) package cream cheese, softened
1 cup powdered sugar
Crystallized ginger slices

Preheat oven to 325F (165C). Grease an 11″ × 7″ baking pan. Line bottom and sides with greased waxed paper, allowing paper to stand 1-inch above sides of pan. Sift flour, salt, Mixed Spice, ginger and baking soda into a bowl. In a saucepan, combine corn syrup, molasses, margarine and brown sugar and heat gently until melted. Stir into flour mixture and add eggs and milk. Stir until evenly mixed.

Pour into prepared pan and bake in pre-heated oven 45 to 50 minutes or until well risen and baked through. Cool in pan, turn out and remove waxed paper. To make icing, put cream cheese into a bowl and soften well. Gradually sift powdered sugar into cream cheese and mix well, using a fork, to make a soft creamy mixture. Spread icing over cold cake. Using blade of a knife, form a rippled effect on icing. Decorate with crystallized ginger. Cut into 12 pieces.

Makes 12 servings.

JAMAICAN CHOCOLATE CAKE

1-½ cups self-rising flour
1-½ teaspoons baking powder
1 teaspoon Mixed Spice, page 8
¾ cup margarine, softened
¾ cup superfine sugar
3 eggs
2 tablespoons unsweetened cocoa powder
2 tablespoons hot water
½ cup granulated sugar
⅔ cup water
2 (2-inch) cinnamon sticks
¼ cup dark rum
2 tablespoons slivered almonds
6 ounces semisweet chocolate, broken in pieces
Whipped cream

Preheat oven to 325F (165C). Generously grease a 5-cup fluted or plain tube pan and dust lightly with flour. Sift flour, baking powder and Mixed Spice into a bowl. Add margarine, superfine sugar and eggs. Blend cocoa powder with hot water and add to flour mixture. Beat well with a wooden spoon 2 minutes or 1 minute if using an electric mixer. Turn mixture into prepared pan. Bake in preheated oven 1-¼ hours or until well risen and cake begins to shrink from edges of pan. Carefully turn out cake onto a wire rack and cool.

Combine granulated sugar and ⅔ cup water in a saucepan. Add cinnamon and heat gently, stirring to dissolve sugar. Boil 5 minutes. Remove from heat, add rum and discard cinnamon. Place cake on a plate. Spoon syrup over cake and let stand 2 hours. Stud top of cake with almonds. Melt choco-late; carefully spoon over cake, spreading to give a smooth even coating. Let stand several hours. Pipe (with a pastry bag) whipped cream around bottom of cake.

Makes 10 to 12 servings.

BRANDY SNAPS

¼ cup butter
¼ cup light-brown sugar
2 tablespoons light corn syrup
½ cup all-purpose flour
Pinch salt
2 pinches Mixed Spice, page 8
½ teaspoon ground ginger
½ teaspoon lemon juice
⅔ cup whipping cream
1 teaspoon powdered sugar
Few drops vanilla extract
24 small strawberries

Preheat oven to 325F (165C). Generously grease 3 baking sheets.

Put butter, brown sugar and syrup in a saucepan and heat gently, stirring until butter has melted and sugar is dissolved. Cool slightly. Sift flour, salt, Mixed Spice and ginger into mixture. Add lemon juice and stir well. Drop teaspoonfuls of mixture onto greased baking sheets, spacing them well apart to allow for spreading. Bake 1 baking sheet at a time in preheated oven 6 to 8 minutes or until golden. Let cool on baking sheet 2 minutes.

Using a palette knife, remove brandy snaps from baking sheet, 1 at a time, and roll around handle of a wooden spoon. Let set and remove from handle. Just before serving, whip cream, powdered sugar and vanilla until thick. Spoon whipped cream into a pastry bag fitted with a small star tube. Pipe whipped cream into ends of each brandy snap. Garnish with strawberries and serve at once. Unfilled Brandy Snaps can be stored in an airtight container up to 2 weeks.

Makes 12 brandy snaps.

GERMAN PEPPER COOKIES

1 egg
½ cup granulated sugar
1 cup all-purpose flour
Pinch salt
½ teaspoon ground cinnamon
¼ teaspoon ground white pepper
¼ teaspoon Mixed Spice, page 8
1 tablespoon cornstarch
½ teaspoon baking powder
Finely grated peel 1 lemon
2 tablespoons chopped mixed candied peel
Powdered sugar, if desired

Whisk egg and granulated sugar until light and fluffy.

Sift flour, salt, cinnamon, white pepper, Mixed Spice, cornstarch and baking powder into egg mixture. Add lemon peel and candied peel and stir well. Chill 1 hour.

Preheat oven to 350F (175C). Lightly grease several baking sheets. Form mixture into 16 small balls and place well apart on baking sheets. Bake in preheated oven 20 minutes or until well risen and lightly golden. Cool on a wire rack. Sprinkle with powdered sugar, if desired. Store several days before serving to allow time for flavors to mellow.

Makes 16 cookies.

SNOWY FLIP

4 eggs, separated
¼ cup superfine sugar
1-¼ cups whipping cream
⅔ cup milk, chilled
1 cup whiskey or brandy
Soda water
1 teaspoon ground mace
Orange and lemon peel to decorate

Place egg whites and egg yolks into separate bowls. Add ½ of sugar to yolks and whisk until pale and creamy. Wash beaters and whisk egg whites until stiff. Add remaining sugar and whisk until stiff.

Add egg whites to yolk mixture and fold in carefully until well mixed and foamy. In a bowl, whip cream until soft peaks form. Fold into egg mixture. Stir in milk and whiskey or brandy. Cover with plastic wrap and chill until required.

Stir gently and divide cream mixture among 8 tall glasses. Fill up each with soda water and sprinkle with mace. Decorate with orange and lemon peel.

Makes 8 servings.

PINA COLADA PUNCH

1 piece dried ginger root, bruised with spoon
1 tablespoon light-brown sugar
1 tablespoon cassia bark, broken in small pieces
⅔ cup water
2 China teabags
⅔ shredded coconut
1-¼ cups boiling water
1-¾ cups pineapple juice
⅔ cup light rum or gin
Crushed ice
Maraschino cherries
Fresh pineapple chuncks
Fresh pineapple leaves, if desired

Put ginger, sugar and cassia bark in a saucepan. Add ⅔ cup water and bring to a boil. Cover and simmer 5 minutes.

Remove from heat and add teabags. Let stand 5 minutes, then strain into a bowl. In a blender or food processor, blend coconut and boiling water 1 minute. Let stand 5 minutes, then strain into tea mixture, pressing coconut to extract all moisture.

Add pineapple juice and chill 1 hour. Add rum or gin and stir well. Serve over crushed ice in tall glasses. Thread cocktail sticks with cherries and pineapple. Add a cocktail stick and swizzle stick to each glass. Garnish with pineapple leaves, if desired.

Makes 4 to 6 servings.

Variation: Add more rum or gin for a stronger flavored drink.

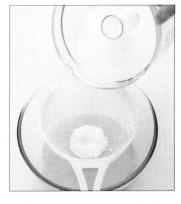

NEGUS

1 bottle ruby port
1 tablespoon light-brown sugar
Finely grated peel 1 lemon
¼ cup lemon juice
¼ teaspoon freshly grated nutmeg
¼ teaspoon ground cinnamon
4 whole cloves
2-½ cups boiling water
Thin strips lemon peel

Pour port into a saucepan and heat gently (do not allow to boil).

Add sugar, lemon peel and juice and spices. Stir well and simmer over a very low heat 10 minutes. Remove cloves.

Add boiling water and serve hot in heatproof glasses. Decorate with lemon peel.

Makes 10 to 12 servings.

HOT MULLED CIDER

1 large cooking apple
14 whole cloves
⅔ cup water
3 (3-inch) cinnamon sticks
6 allspice berries
¼ teaspoon freshly grated nutmeg
2 tablespoons light-brown sugar
4 cups medium dry cider
2 tablespoons butter
Red apple slices
Fresh mint sprigs, if desired

Stud cooking apple with cloves. Cut apple in half and place, cut-sides down, in a saucepan. Add water, cinnamon, allspice, nutmeg and brown sugar.

Cover and simmer gently 20 minutes. Strain into a pan. Remove spices and press cooked apple through a sieve into pan.

Add cider and butter and heat through gently. Serve hot in heatproof glasses. Garnish with red apple slices and mint sprigs, if desired.

Makes 8 to 10 servings.

GINGER BEER

Finely grated peel and juice 1 large lemon
5 teaspons cream of tartar
2 cups sugar
1 (1-inch) piece fresh ginger root (1 oz.), peeled
3 to 4 tablespoons dried ginger root (1 oz.)
8 cups boiling water
8 cups cold water
1 tablespon cake compressed yeast
1 slice toast

Place lemon peel, cream of tartar and sugar in a large bowl or clean plastic bucket. Crush fresh and dried ginger root with a rolling pin and add to bowl.

Cover with boiling water and stir well until sugar dissolves. Add cold water and lemon juice and stir well. Spread yeast on toast and float (yeast-side down) on mixture. Cover with a clean cloth and let stand in a warm place 24 hours.

Strain ginger beer through muslin. Pour into clean plastic bottles, filling each half-full (this allows room for mixture to effervesce upon opening). Screw lids on tightly and let stand in a cool place 2 to 3 days. Open each bottle to allow excess air to escape and replace lids. Drink Ginger Beer within 2 weeks.

Makes 15 to 20 servings.

NOTE: To crush dried ginger root, place in a plastic bag and crush with a rolling pin on a flat surface. To serve, garnish with fresh mint sprigs. lemon pieces and lemon peel strips, if desired.

SHERBERT

1-¾ cups water
1 cup sugar
2 (3-inch) cinnamon sticks
½ teaspoon whole cloves
8 green cardamoms, lightly crushed
3 lemon peel strips
½ teaspoon rose water
1 to 2 drops red food coloring, if desired
Ice cold water
Lemon peel curls
Rose petals

Pour water into a saucepan. Add sugar, cinnamon, cloves, cardamoms and lemon peel. Heat gently, stirring to dissolve sugar.

Bring to a boil, then reduce heat and simmer gently 20 to 30 minutes or until mixture is thickened and syrupy. Remove from heat.

Stir in rose water and food coloring, if desired. Strain and cool, then dilute with ice cold water. Serve in glasses, garnished with lemon peel and rose petals.

Makes 6 to 8 servings.

SWEET LASSI

AUSTRIAN CHOCOLATE CUP

1-¾ cups plain yogurt
4 ice cubes
1-¼ cups ice cold water
2 teaspoons lemon juice
2 tablespoons sugar
Ice cubes
½ teaspoon cumin seeds, crushed
Lemon slices
Fresh mint sprig, if desired

In a blender or food processor, blend yogurt, 4 ice cubes and ice cold water 30 seconds.

Add lemon juice and sugar and blend mixture again until thoroughly combined.

Pour mixture over ice cubes in glasses and sprinkle with crushed cumin seeds.
Garnish with lemon slices and mint sprig, if desired.

Makes 6 servings.

3 ounces semisweet chocolate, broken in pieces
Finely grated peel 1 small orange
¼ teaspoon ground cinnamon
1-½ cups milk
¼ cup whipping cream
Grated chocolate
2 to 3 (3-inch) cinnamon sticks

Combine chocolate, orange peel, cinnamon and 3 tablespoons of milk in a saucepan and heat very gently until chocolate melts, stirring frequently.

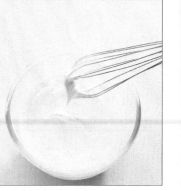

Add remaining milk and heat through gently until piping hot, stirring frequently. Whisk whipping cream until soft peaks form.

Pour hot chocolate into mugs or heatproof glasses. Top with whipped cream. Sprinkle with grated chocolate and add a cinnamon stick to each one for stirring.

Makes 2 to 3 servings.

NOTE: Wind a curly strip of orange peel around cinnamon sticks for a pretty effect, if desired.

CURRIES, INDIAN AND OTHER SPICY FOODS

THE CULTURAL INFLUENCES

Indian Food encompasses the cooking of many different regions – the country itself is huge, over a million square miles – and the foods are quite different from state to state. Geography and local produce both play a part in forming the diverse regional traditions.

In the north, where the climate is temperate, sheep are reared – and the dishes are generally cooked slowly in the oven. Travelling south through Dehli and the Punjab, the diet becomes much richer – here they cook mainly with ghee (a clarified butter) and eat both goat and chicken. In these northern regions, instead of rice, the preference is for breads such as chapatis and parathas.

To the east around the Bay of Bengal, there is an abundance of fish from the many rivers and, of course, from the bay itself. Coconut palms grow in the hot and humid climate, so coconut also features strongly in many of their recipes. On the west coast, in Gujarat, the people are mainly vegetarian, eating lots of beans and peas as well as vegetables and in Tamil Nadu in the far south-east, the people are also vegetarian.

The humid tropical conditions of the southwest, in Goa and Malabar, mean that date and coconut palms, and banana plants flourish. Here there is also plenty of fish and shellfish. Southern Indians eat more rice than the northerners and they prefer to steam foods – the dishes are traditionally very hot, much more so than in the north.

Influence of Race & Religion

India is a country of vastly varied races and religions – and it is religion that influences diet to the greatest extent. There are hundreds of different religions, some original, others imported over the centuries by conquering peoples from other lands, each with its own customs and taboos. For instance, Moslems and Jews don't eat pork, while Hindus and Sikhs are prohibited from eating beef – and although many Hindus are strict vegetarians, others eat fish and shellfish, classing these as a harvest from the seas. The taboos don't just cover meats – Kashmiri Hindus also don't eat onions or garlic, or vegetables or fruit that resemble meaty colors such as beets, tomatoes or watermelon.

Use of Spices

The imaginative use of spices sets Indian cooking apart from other cuisines – it is by far the most aromatic of all types of cooking – and perhaps the most pleasant discovery one can make about it is that although always spicy, the food isn't necessarily hot. In fact, chiles – which make the food hot – were only introduced to India in the 16th century.

Red chiles are milder than green, and larger chiles generally milder than small ones and unless you like very hot food, the seeds of all types are best removed. Be careful when handling chiles and always wash your hands afterwards to prevent irritation.

Other spices can add warmth in different degrees – mustard seeds, black pepper and cayenne pepper are all quite hot, while ground ginger, nutmeg and cardamom are warm. Warm and hot spices feature more in the winter months because they generate heat in the body, while the cooler spices such as fennel, cloves and green cardamom are used in summer drinks and desserts.

The cornerstone of Indian cooking is the spice mixtures – or masalas. Spices release their flavor when they are crushed and traditionally the spices are ground by hand on a grinding stone with a pestle. At home, a mortar and pestle works very well for small quantities. However, if you have an electric coffee grinder, you will be able to make spice grinding easy.

The most common spices are cumin, coriander seeds and mustard seeds, black pepper, ground turmeric, cinnamon, cardamom and cloves. Whole spices have a more intense flavor that lasts much longer. Buy small quantities and store them in an airtight container in a cool place. Whole spices will stay fresh from one to three years, while ground spices are really fresh for up to three months.

SPICE MIXES & COCONUT MILK

NUT MASALA
2 tablespoons vegetable oil
1 teaspoon cumin seeds
1 teaspoon cardamom seeds
1 tablespoon poppy seeds
1 teaspoon black peppercorns
2 garlic cloves, crushed
1 (1-inch) piece fresh gingerroot, grated
2 oz. blanched almonds or unsalted cashew nuts, chopped
¼ cup boiling water

Heat oil in a heavy skillet, add spices and cook over medium heat 5 to 10 minutes, until golden brown, stirring constantly. Add garlic and gingerroot and cook 2 minutes more, then cool.

Put spice mixture in a blender or food processor fitted with the metal blade. Add almonds or cashew nuts and water; grind to a smooth paste. Cover tightly and keep in a cool place for up to 1 month.

TANDOORI MASALA
1 tablespoon cumin seeds
1 tablespoon coriander seeds
1 tablespoon red (cayenne) pepper
Few drops of red food coloring

Grind cumin and coriander seeds to a fine powder in a coffee grinder or with a pestle and mortar. Stir in cayenne and food coloring and mix well. Store in a small airtight jar up to 2 months.

MOGHUL MASALA
Seeds from 2 oz. (¼ cup) green cardamom pods
2 (3-inch) cinnamon sticks, crushed
1 tablespoon whole cloves
1 tablespoon black peppercorns
1 teaspoon grated nutmeg

Grind spices to a fine powder in a coffee grinder or with a pestle and mortar. Store in a small, airtight jar up to 2 months.

GARAM MASALA
1 tablespoon plus 1 teaspoon cardamom seeds
2 (3-inch) cinnamon sticks, crushed
2 teaspoons whole cloves
1 tablespoon plus 1 teaspoon black peppercorns
3 tablespoons cumin seeds
3 tablespoons coriander seeds

Put all spices in a heavy skillet and dry roast over medium heat 5 to 10 minutes, until browned, stirring constantly. Cool completely, then grind to a fine powder in a coffee grinder or with a pestle and mortar. Store in an airtight jar up to 2 months.

HOT SPICE MIX
¼ cup cumin seeds
8 dried red chiles
1 tablespoon black peppercorns
1 tablespoon cardamom seeds
1 (3-inch) cinnamon stick, crushed
1 tablespoon plus 1 teaspoon black mustard seeds
1 tablespoon fenugreek seeds

Put all spices in a heavy skillet and dry roast over medium heat 5 to 10 minutes, until browned, stirring constantly. Cool completely, then grind to a fine powder in a coffee grinder or with a pestle and mortar. Store in an airtight jar up to 2 months.

COCONUT MILK
1 cup dried shredded coconut
2 cups hot water

Put coconut and water in a blender or food processor fitted with the metal blade; process 1 minute. Strain through a fine sieve, pressing out as much liquid as possible, then discard coconut.

Makes about 2 cups.

— MURGHAL MASALA CHOPS —

— SKEWERED BEEF KABOBS —

8 lamb loin chops
1 tablespoon Murghal Masala, page 51
¼ teaspoon chile powder
1 garlic clove, crushed
1 tablespoon lemon juice
Chicory and cherry tomatoes, to garnish

Wipe lamb chops with a damp paper towel; trim off any excess fat. Slash meaty parts two or three times on each side and set aside.

1½ pounds lean ground beef
1 onion, finely chopped
1 (2-inch) piece fresh gingerroot, grated
3 garlic cloves, crushed
1 teaspoon chile powder
1 tablespoon Garam Masala, page 51
1 tablespoon chopped cilantro (fresh coriander)
1 tablespoon ground almonds
1 egg, beaten
¼ cup garbanzo bean flour
6 tablespoons plain yogurt
2 teaspoons vegetable oil
Onion rings and thin lemon wedges, to garnish

Put Murghal Masala, chile powder, garlic and lemon juice in a small bowl; mix to a smooth paste. Rub paste into chops, cover and refrigerate 2 to 3 hours to allow meat to absorb flavors.

Mix together beef, onion, gingerroot, garlic, spices, cilantro, almonds, egg and flour in a large bowl. Cover beef mixture and refrigerate up to 4 hours to allow flavors to blend. Shape into 16 to 20 ovals; thread onto four long skewers. Mix together yogurt and oil and brush over kabobs.

Preheat broiler or grill. Place chops on a grill rack and cook 12 to 15 minutes, until browned on outside and just pink in center, turning over halfway through cooking. Press point of a sharp knife into center of chops – when they are ready, juices will be just faintly pink. Serve hot, garnished with chicory and tomatoes.

Makes 4 servings.

Preheat broiler or grill. Cook kabobs 20 to 25 minutes, until well browned and no longer pink in center. Baste kabobs with more of the yogurt and oil mixture and turn occasionally during cooking. Serve hot, garnished with onion rings and lemon wedges.

Makes 4 servings.

NOTE: The meatball mixture can be made up to 12 hours in advance and refrigerated.

LAMB TIKKA

1 (2-lb.) boneless leg of lamb
1 teaspoon ground cumin
¾ teaspoon ground turmeric
Salt to taste
6 tablespoons plain yogurt
½ small onion, finely chopped
1 (2-inch) piece fresh gingerroot, grated
2 garlic cloves, crushed
Few drops red food coloring, optional
1 teaspoon Garam Masala, page 51

Trim fat from lamb; cut lamb into 1½-inch cubes. Put lamb cubes in a bowl; add cumin, turmeric, salt, yogurt, onion, gingerroot and garlic.

Mix together well, then, if you wish, add enough coloring to give mixture a red tint. Cover and refrigerate 4 to 6 hours. Drain lamb from marinade and thread cubes onto eight short skewers, pressing cubes closely together.

Preheat broiler or grill. Cook kabobs 15 to 20 minutes, or until done, basting kabobs with any remaining marinade and turning occasionally during cooking. The lamb is ready when it is browned on the outside and still slightly pink in the center. Sprinkle with Garam Masala and serve at once.

Makes 4 servings.

KASHMIR MEATBALL CURRY

1½ pounds ground lamb
¼ cup garbanzo bean flour
3 tablespoons Garam Masala, page 51
¼ teaspoon red (cayenne) pepper
Salt to taste
6 tablespoons plain yogurt
2 tablespoons vegetable oil
1 (3-inch) cinnamon stick
6 green cardamom pods, bruised
2 fresh bay leaves
6 whole cloves
1 (2-inch) piece fresh gingerroot, grated
1 cup water
2 tablespoons chopped cilantro (fresh coriander), to garnish

Put lamb, flour, Garam Masala, cayenne, salt and half the yogurt in a bowl; mix together well. Shape into 16 long ovals. Heat oil in a shallow heavy saucepan, add cinnamon, cardamom pods, bay leaves and cloves. Stir-fry a few seconds, then add meatballs; cook until lightly browned on all sides. Add gingerroot; cook a few seconds more. Stir remaining yogurt into water; pour over meatballs.

Cover pan and bring to a boil. Reduce heat and simmer about 30 minutes, until meatballs are cooked and almost all the sauce has been absorbed, stirring gently two or three times. Sprinkle with cilantro and serve at once.

Makes 4 servings.

NOTE: If meatballs release a lot of fat during initial cooking, drain off fat before adding yogurt liquid.

LAMB KORMA

1½ pounds boneless leg of lamb
¼ cup vegetable oil
1 large onion, finely chopped
1 recipe Nut Masala, made with cashews, page 51
2 tablespoons Garam Masala, page 51
3 dried red chiles, seeded, crushed
1 (1-inch) piece fresh gingerroot, grated
1 tablespoon chopped cilantro (fresh coriander)
1 cup half and half
⅓ cup water
Salt to taste
2 teaspoons lemon juice
Cilantro (fresh coriander) leaves and lemon wedges,
to garnish

Wipe lamb with a damp paper towel, trim off excess fat and cut lamb into 2-inch cubes.

Heat oil in a heavy saucepan, add lamb and cook until browned all over. Add onion and cook about 5 minutes to soften, stirring frequently. Stir in masalas, chiles and gingerroot; cook 2 minutes more.

Add chopped cilantro, half and half, water and salt. Bring to a boil. Reduce heat, cover and simmer about 1 hour, or until lamb is tender. Stir in lemon juice. Serve hot, garnished with cilantro and lemon wedges.

Makes 4 servings.

MADRAS MEAT CURRY

1½ pounds beef round steak
2 tablespoons vegetable oil
1 large onion, finely sliced
4 whole cloves
4 green cardamom pods, bruised
3 green chiles, seeded, finely chopped
2 dry red chiles, seeded, crushed
1 (1-inch) piece fresh gingerroot, grated
2 garlic cloves, crushed
2 teaspoons ground coriander
2 teaspoons ground turmeric
¼ cup water
¼ cup tamarind nectar, see note below
Salt to taste
Lettuce leaves, to garnish

Cut beef into 1-inch cubes. Heat oil in a large heavy saucepan, add beef and cook until browned all over. Remove with a slotted spoon and set aside. Add onion, cloves and cardamom to pan; cook, stirring, about 8 minutes, until onion is soft and golden brown. Stir in chiles, gingerroot, garlic, coriander and turmeric; cook 2 minutes. Return beef to pan, add water and cover. Simmer 1 hour.

Stir in tamarind nectar and salt; simmer another 20 to 30 minutes, until beef is tender. Serve, garnished with lettuce leaves.

Makes 4 servings.

NOTE: Tamarind nectar: soak a walnut-sized piece of tamarind paste in 1 cup boiling water about 20 minutes, then squeeze in cheesecloth to extract liquid, discard pulp. Store in refrigerator up to 1 week. Tamarind nectar is also available commercially.

LAMB WITH ONIONS

1½ pounds lamb shoulder
1 teaspoon ground turmeric
1 teaspoon ground cumin
1 teaspoon ground coriander
1 (1-inch) piece fresh gingerroot, grated
2 garlic cloves, crushed
3 tablespoons vegetable oil
1 tablespoon superfine sugar
4 large onions, sliced into thin rings
1 lb. potatoes, cut into large chunks
1 cup water
Salt and red (cayenne) pepper to taste
1 teaspoon Garam Masala, page 51
Rosemary sprigs, to garnish

Wipe lamb with a damp paper towel, trim off excess fat and cut into 1½ inch cubes.

Put lamb in a non-metal bowl. Mix together turmeric, cumin, coriander, gingerroot and garlic; add to lamb. Stir well, then cover loosely and refrigerate 2 to 3 hours. Heat oil in a heavy saucepan until smoking. Stir in sugar, then add onions and cook over medium-high heat 10 minutes, until a rich brown, stirring frequently. Remove onions with a slotted spoon and set aside.

Add lamb to pan; cook until browned all over. Add potatoes and cook, stirring, 2 minutes. Return onions to pan; add water, salt and cayenne. Bring to a boil. Reduce heat, cover and simmer 1¼ hours, or until lamb is tender, stirring occasionally. Stir in Garam Masala and serve, garnished with rosemary sprigs.

Makes 4 servings.

ROAST LAMB & PISTACHIOS

1 (3½ to 4 lb.) leg of lamb, boned, rolled and tied
2 garlic cloves, crushed
1 (1-inch) piece fresh gingerroot, grated
1 teaspoon ground cumin
2 teaspoons Murghal Masala, page 51
Salt and red (cayenne) pepper to taste
¾ cup shelled pistachios
2 tablespoons lemon juice
2 tablespoons brown sugar
½ cup plain yogurt
⅔ cup water
2 pinches saffron threads
2 tablespoons boiling water
1 tablespoon cornstarch
2 tablespoons shelled pistachios, sliced, to garnish

Prick lamb all over with point of a knife, place in a large non-metal casserole dish. Put garlic, gingerroot, cumin, Murghal Masala, salt, cayenne, pistachios, lemon juice, sugar and yogurt in a blender or food processor fitted with the metal blade; process until smooth. Pour over lamb. Cover and refrigerate 24 hours, turning lamb occasionally. Preheat oven to 350F (175C). Add water to lamb; bring to a boil.

Cover tightly and cook in oven 1½ hours. Reduce heat to 300F (150C); cook another 30 minutes. Turn off oven and leave 30 minutes. Meanwhile soak saffron in boiling water 20 minutes, then blend in cornstarch. Remove lamb and keep warm. Skim excess fat from sauce; pour sauce into a saucepan. Add saffron mixture; cook, stirring, until boiling and thickened. Slice lamb, pour a little sauce over and garnish with pistachios. Serve remaining sauce separately.

Makes 6 to 8 servings.

PORK IN SPINACH SAUCE

1½ pounds fresh spinach
Salt to taste
1½ pounds lean boneless pork
3 tablespoons vegetable oil
2 onions, finely sliced
4 garlic cloves, crushed
1 (1-inch) piece fresh gingerroot, grated
3 tablespoons Garam Masala, page 51
½ teaspoon ground turmeric
1 bay leaf
2 tomatoes, peeled, chopped
2 green chiles, seeded, chopped
⅔ cup plain yogurt
1⅔ cups water
Sliced tomato and bay leaves, to garnish

Trim stems from spinach and cook leaves in boiling salted water 2 to 3 minutes until tender. Drain thoroughly and rinse under cold running water. Put in a blender or food processor fitted with the metal blade; process to a smooth puree. Set aside. Preheat oven to 325F (160C). Cut pork into 1-inch cubes. Heat oil in a large skillet and fry pork until browned all over. Transfer to a casserole dish using a slotted spoon.

Add onions to pan and cook, stirring, 10 to 15 minutes, until a rich brown. Add garlic, gingerroot, Garam Masala, turmeric, bay leaf, tomatoes and chiles. Cook, stirring 2 to 3 minutes, until tomatoes are softened. Add yogurt and water and stir well. Pour over pork, cover and bake 1¼ to 1½ hours, until pork is tender. Remove bay leaf, stir in spinach and salt, re-cover and bake another 10 minutes. Serve hot, garnished with tomatoes and bay leaves.

Makes 4 servings.

LAMB WITH CAULIFLOWER

1½ pounds lean lamb
3 tablespoons vegetable oil
2 onions, finely chopped
1 (1-inch) piece fresh gingerroot, grated
4 garlic cloves, crushed
2 tablespoons Hot Spice Mix, page 51
1¼ cups beef stock
Salt to taste
1 small cauliflower, cut into flowerets
1 teaspoon Garam Masala, page 51
2 teaspoons lime juice
Lime slices, to garnish

Trim excess fat from lamb; cut into 1-inch cubes. set aside.

Heat oil in a large heavy saucepan; add onions. Cook over medium heat 5 minutes, until soft, stirring frequently. Stir in gingerroot, garlic and spice mix; cook 1 minute. Add lamb; cook until browned all over.

Stir in stock and salt; bring to a boil. Cover and simmer 25 minutes. Add cauliflowerets; cook another 5 to 10 minutes, until lamb and cauliflower are tender, stirring occasionally. Sprinkle in Garam Masala and lime juice and stir gently. Serve hot, garnished with lime slices.

Makes 4 servings.

CHICKEN IN GINGER SAUCE

ROAST DUCK IN FRUIT SAUCE

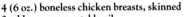

4 (6 oz.) boneless chicken breasts, skinned
2 tablespoons vegetable oil
6 green onions, finely chopped
3 garlic cloves, crushed
1 (2-inch) piece fresh gingerroot, grated
1 teaspoon ground cumin
2 teaspoons Garam Masala, page 51
Salt and pepper to taste
1 tablespoon lemon juice
6 tablespoons hot water
Parsley sprigs and lemon slice, to garnish

1 (4½ lb.) duck
3 onions, chopped
1 cup chopped mixed nuts
1 cup fresh bread crumbs
4 tablespoons chopped cilantro (fresh coriander)
Salt and red (cayenne) pepper, to taste
1 egg yolk
1 tablespoon Garam Masala, page 51
2 tablespoons vegetable oil
2 garlic cloves, crushed
1 (1-inch) piece fresh gingerroot, grated
1 teaspoon ground turmeric
2 tablespoons ground coriander
1 teaspoon garbanzo bean flour
1¼ cups plain yogurt
Juice of 2 lemons and 2 oranges

Rinse chicken, pat dry with paper towels and slice thinly.

Heat oil in a large skillet, add onions and cook 2 to 3 minutes, to soften, stirring. Remove from pan with a slotted spoon. Add chicken to pan and cook over high heat, stirring frequently, for about 5 minutes, or until browned all over.

Preheat oven to 375F (190C). Rinse duck, pat dry with paper towels, then prick skin with a fork. In a bowl, mix together 1 onion, nuts, bread crumbs, 3 tablespoons cilantro, salt, cayenne pepper and egg yolk. Stuff duck with mixture, then truss neatly. Rub Garam Masala into skin; place duck in a roasting pan. Roast 1¼ hours, or until tender, spoon off fat from pan as it accumulates. Remove duck and keep warm. Heat oil in a saucepan, add remaining onions and cook, stirring, 5 minutes, until soft.

Stir in garlic, gingerroot, cumin, Garam Masala, salt and pepper. Cook 1 minute, then stir in cooked onions, lemon juice and water. Cover and cook over low heat about 10 minutes, or until chicken is tender. Serve hot, garnished with parsley and lemon.

Makes 4 servings.

Stir in garlic, gingerroot, turmeric, ground coriander, salt, cayenne and flour. Cook 1 minute, then stir in yogurt. Simmer 10 minutes, then stir in lemon juice and orange juice and heat gently, without boiling. Carve duck. Arrange on a platter; pour sauce over duck and sprinkle with remaining 1 tablespoon cilantro. Serve hot.

Makes 4 servings.

NOTE: This looks very attractive garnished with spirals of orange and lemon peel.

LEMON & CORIANDER CHICKEN

4 chicken thighs, skinned
4 chicken drumsticks, skinned
¼ cup vegetable oil
1 (2-inch) piece fresh gingerroot, grated
4 garlic cloves, crushed
1 green chile, seeded, finely chopped
½ teaspoon ground turmeric
1 teaspoon ground cumin
1 teaspoon ground coriander
Salt and red (cayenne) pepper to taste
½ cup water
Grated peel and juice of 1 lemon
4 oz. cilantro (fresh coriander), chopped
Cilantro (fresh coriander) leaves and lemon
   slices, to garnish

Rinse chicken; pat dry with paper towels. Heat oil in a large skillet and add chicken. Fry, turning frequently, until browned all over. Remove from pan with a slotted spoon; set aside. Add gingerroot and garlic to skillet; cook 1 minute. Stir in chile, turmeric, cumin, coriander, salt and cayenne; cook 1 minute more.

Return chicken to pan, add water and lemon peel and juice. Bring to a boil, then cover and cook over medium heat 25 to 30 minutes, or until chicken is tender. Stir in chopped cilantro. Serve hot, garnished with cilantro leaves and lemon slices.

Makes 4 servings.

VARIATION: Substitute fresh parsley, or a mixture of parsley and mint for the cilantro, if preferred.

APRICOT & CHICKEN CURRY

2½ lbs. chicken pieces, skinned
½ teaspoon chile powder
1 tablespoon Garam Masala, page 51
1 (1-inch) piece fresh gingerroot, grated
2 garlic cloves, crushed
1 cup dried apricots
⅔ cup water
2 tablespoons vegetable oil
2 onions, finely sliced
1 (14-oz.) can chopped tomatoes
Salt to taste
1 tablespoon sugar
2 tablespoons white wine vinegar

Rinse chicken; pat dry with paper towels. Cut each piece into four pieces and put in a large bowl. Add chile powder, Garam Masala, gingerroot and garlic; toss well to coat chicken pieces. Cover and refrigerate 2 to 3 hours to allow chicken to absorb flavors. In a separate bowl, combine apricots and water; soak 2 to 3 hours.

Heat oil in a large heavy saucepan; add chicken pieces. Cook over high heat about 5 minutes, or until browned all over. Remove from pan and set aside. Add onions to pan and cook, stirring, about 5 minutes, until soft. Return chicken to pan with tomatoes, cover and cook over low heat 20 minutes. Drain apricots, add to pan with salt, sugar and vinegar. Simmer, covered, 10 to 15 minutes, until tender. Serve hot.

Makes 4 servings.

TANDOORI CHICKEN

2½ lbs. chicken pieces
1 tablespoon lime juice
Salt to taste
1 small onion
1 tablespoon Tandoori Masala, page 51
2 teaspoons Garam Masala, page 51
1 (1-inch) piece fresh gingerroot, grated
1¼ cups plain yogurt
Cilantro (fresh coriander) and lime wedges to garnish

Rinse chicken pieces, pat dry with paper towels, then slash meaty parts two or three times.

Place chicken in a shallow non-metal dish. Sprinkle with lime juice and salt. Set aside. Put onion, masalas, gingerroot, salt and yogurt into a blender or food processor fitted with the metal blade; process until smooth and frothy. Pour over chicken and cover loosely. Marinate in the refrigerator 6 hours, or overnight.

Preheat oven to 400F (205C). Drain excess marinade from chicken pieces; place them in a roasting pan. Cook 25 to 30 minutes, until tender and well browned. Serve hot, garnished with cilantro and lime wedges.

Makes 4 servings.

NOTE: If preferred, use a 3½ pound roasting chicken and cook for about 1¼ hours, or until juices run clear, when thigh is pierced with a knife.

SPICY CHICKEN PATTIES

1¼ lbs. boneless chicken breasts, skinned
4 green onions, finely chopped
3 tomatoes, peeled, seeded, chopped
3 tablespoons chopped cilantro (fresh coriander)
1 (1-inch) piece fresh gingerroot, grated
1 garlic clove, crushed
1 teaspoon ground cumin
1 teaspoon Garam Masala, page 51
Salt and red (cayenne) pepper to taste
1 egg, beaten
1½ cups fresh bread crumbs
¼ cup vegetable oil
Tomato wedges and green onion brushes, to garnish

Rinse chicken breasts; pat dry with paper towels. Finely mince chicken and put into a large bowl with onions, tomatoes, cilantro, gingerroot, garlic, cumin, Garam Masala, salt, cayenne, egg and half of the bread crumbs. Mix thoroughly, then divide into 18 pieces and form into patties. Roll patties in remaining bread crumbs, to coat completely.

Heat oil in a large skillet. Fry patties in two or three batches 10 to 12 minutes, until crisp and golden brown and no longer pink in center. Drain on paper towels. Serve hot, garnished with tomato wedges and green onion brushes.

Makes 6 servings.

VARIATION: Use boneless turkey breast instead of chicken, if preferred.

NOTE: Patties can be prepared up to 12 hours in advance, chill until ready to cook.

SPICY BEEF LETTUCE CUPS

CHICKEN BIRIANI

12 ounces boneless sirloin steak, trimmed
2 tablespoons light soy sauce
1 tablespoon dry sherry
1 (½-inch) piece ginger root, peeled, grated
1 clove garlic, crushed
2 pinches Five Spice Powder
1 teaspoon chile sauce
2 tablespoons corn oil
6 green onions, sliced diagonally
1 small red bell pepper, seeded, diced
½ teaspoon cornstarch
1 teaspoon water
8 crisp lettuce cups, chilled
Fresh parsley sprigs, if desired

Cut steak in very thin slivers and place in a bowl.

Add soy sauce, sherry, ginger, garlic, Five Spice Powder and chile sauce; mix well. Cover and refrigerate 1 hour, stirring occasionally. Heat oil in a skillet or wok. Add onions and red pepper; stir-fry 1 minute.

Add beef mixture to onion mixture and stir-fry 2 to 3 minutes. In a custard cup, blend cornstarch and water until smooth; add to beef mixture. Cook 1 minute, stirring constantly. Spoon beef mixture into lettuce cups. Garnish with parsley sprigs, if desired.

Makes 4 servings.

1¼ lbs. boneless chicken breasts, skinned
6 tablespoons vegetable oil
6 green cardamom pods, bruised
½ teaspoon cumin seeds
2 onions, finely sliced
4 garlic cloves, crushed
1 (2-inch) piece fresh gingerroot, grated
⅔ cup plain yogurt
½ cup water
3 cups basmati rice, washed
Salt and ground black pepper to taste
Large pinch of saffron threads
2 tablespoons boiling water
2 tablespoons cold water
Few drops red food coloring
3 tablespoons sliced almonds, toasted, and
  2 tablespoons raisins, to garnish

Cut chicken into ¾-inch cubes. Set aside. Soak rice in cold water 30 minutes, then drain. Heat 4 tablespoons oil in a large heavy saucepan, add cardamom pods and cumin seeds and fry 1 minute. Stir in onions, garlic, gingerroot and chicken; cook about 5 minutes, stirring over high heat, until chicken is browned all over. Stir in yogurt 1 tablespoon at a time, then add ½ cup water. Reduce heat, cover and simmer 15 minutes.

Heat remaining oil in a separate pan, stir in rice and fry 2 to 3 minutes, until golden, stirring constantly. Stir into chicken mixture with salt and pepper. Cover and simmer 12 to 15 minutes, until rice and chicken are tender. Soak saffron in boiling water 5 minutes. Add cold water to food coloring. Pour saffron liquid and red mixture into separate ⅓ sections of rice and stir in to color rice yellow and red, leaving ⅓ white. Serve hot, garnished with almonds and raisins.

Makes 4 servings.

GOLDEN STEAMED CHICKEN

DUCK WITH HONEY & LIME

1 (3½-lb.) chicken
¾ cup basmati rice
3 tablespoons vegetable oil
½ teaspoon chile powder
⅓ cup raisins
½ cup sliced almonds
1 tablespoon chopped fresh thyme
¾ cup water
Salt to taste
½ teaspoon ground cumin
½ teaspoon ground turmeric
1 teaspoon ground cilantro
2 teaspoon Garam Masala, page 51
Salt and pepper (cayenne) to taste
½ cup hot water
Thyme sprigs, to garnish

Rinse chicken, pat dry with paper towels and set aside. Wash rice thoroughly and soak in cold water 30 minutes, then drain. Heat 1 tablespoon oil in a saucepan, add rice and fry, stirring 2 to 3 minutes, until golden brown. Stir in chile powder, rasisins, almonds, thyme, ¾ cup water and salt. Bring to a boil, then reduce heat, cover and simmer 10 to 15 minutes, until rice has absorbed all the liquid. Cool completely. Stuff chicken with rice.

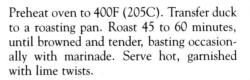

Truss chicken neatly, then place in a steamer and steam 1 hour. Heat remaining oil in a large saucepan. Add cumin, turmeric, coriander, Garam Masala, salt and cayenne; cook 1 minute. Transfer chicken to this pan and cook 5 minutes, turning chicken with two wooden spoons until well coated in spice mixture. Pour hot water down side of pan, cover and cook over low heat 15 to 20 minutes, until chicken is tender. Serve hot, garnished with thyme sprigs.

Makes 4 servings.

4 (8-oz.) duck quarters, skinned
2 tablespoons vegetable oil
1 onion, finely chopped
2 garlic cloves, crushed
1 (1-inch) piece fresh gingerroot, finely sliced
8 green cardamom pods, bruised
1 (3-inch) cinnamon stick
3 tablespoons honey
Juice of 2 limes
Twists of lime, to garnish

Rinse duck; pat dry with paper towels. Slash meaty parts two or three times.

Place duck in a shallow non-metal dish. Set aside. Heat oil in a skillet, add onion and cook, stirring, until soft. Stir in garlic, gingerroot, cardamom pods and cinnamon and cook 2 minutes more. Stir in honey and lime juice, then pour over duck. Cover and refrigerate 2 to 3 hours.

Preheat oven to 400F (205C). Transfer duck to a roasting pan. Roast 45 to 60 minutes, until browned and tender, basting occasionally with marinade. Serve hot, garnished with lime twists.

Makes 4 servings.

MOGHUL SHREDDED DUCK

1 lb. boneless duck breasts, skinned
4 tablespoons vegetable oil
1 onion, finely chopped
1 recipe Nut Masala made with ¾ cup cashew nuts,
    page 51
1 teaspoon ground turmeric
⅔ cup shredded coconut
½ cup raisins
⅔ cup plain yogurt
6 tablespoons whipping cream
⅓ cup unsalted cashew nuts
1 green chile, seeded, chopped

Rinse duck breasts; pat dry with paper towels.

Slice duck into ¼-inch-thick strips. Heat 3 tablespoons oil in a large skillet, add duck and cook over high heat about 5 minutes, until browned all over. Remove duck from pan with a slotted spoon and set aside. Add onion to pan and cook, stirring, 5 minutes, or until soft. Stir in Nut Masala and turmeric; cook 2 minutes. Stir in coconut, raisins, yogurt, cream and duck.

Cover and cook over low heat 15 to 20 minutes, until duck is tender, stirring occasionally. Just before serving, heat remaining oil in a small pan, add cashew nuts and fry 2 to 3 minutes, until golden. Add chile and fry 1 minute more. Transfer duck to a warm serving dish, spoon over cashew nut and chile mixture. Serve hot.

Makes 4 to 6 servings.

CHICKEN WITH LENTILS

8 oz. boneless chicken breasts
1¼ cups red split lentils
3 cups water
½ teaspoon ground turmeric
4 tablespoons vegetable oil
6 green cardamom pods, bruised
1 onion, finely sliced
1 (½-inch) piece fresh gingerroot, grated
Salt and red (cayenne) pepper to taste
2 tablespoons lemon juice
⅔ cup water
1 teaspoon cumin seeds
2 garlic cloves, finely sliced

Rinse chicken, pat dry with paper towels and cut into cubes. Set aside.

Wash lentils, place in a large saucepan and add 3 cups water and turmeric. Bring to a boil, then reduce heat, cover and simmer 20 to 30 minutes, or until tender. Drain thoroughly. Meanwhile, heat half the oil in a large saucepan, add cardamom pods and fry 1 minute. Add onion and fry, stirring frequently, about 8 minutes, until golden brown. Add chicken and fry 5 minutes, until browned all over. Add gingerroot and fry 1 minute more. Season with salt and cayenne.

Stir in lemon juice and ⅔ cup water. Cover and simmer 25 to 30 minutes, or until chicken is tender. Stir in lentil mixture and cook, stirring, 5 minutes more. Meanwhile, heat remaining oil in a small pan, add cumin seeds and garlic and fry, stirring, over medium heat 1 to 2 minutes, until garlic is golden. Transfer chicken and lentil mixture to a serving dish and pour garlic mixture over the top. Serve hot.

Makes 4 servings.

CHICKEN IN SPICY SAUCE

CURRIED CHICKEN LIVERS

8 chicken thighs, skinned
1 (8-oz.) can tomatoes, drained
2 tablespoons tomato paste
2 tablespoons chile sauce
2 teaspoons sugar
1 tablespoon Garam Masala, page 51
2 tablespoons light soy sauce
1 (2-inch) piece fresh gingerroot, grated
2 garlic cloves, crushed
Juice of 1 lime and 1 lemon
Twists of lime peel and lemon peel, to garnish

Rinse chicken; pat dry with paper towels. Slash meaty parts of chicken two or three times.

Place chicken in a shallow non-metal dish and set aside. Put tomatoes, tomato paste, chile sauce, sugar, Garam Masala, soy sauce, gingerroot, garlic, lime juice and lemon juice in a blender or food processor fitted with the metal blade; process until pureed. Pour over chicken, cover and refrigerate 2 to 3 hours to allow chicken to absorb flavors.

Preheat oven to 375F (190C). Put chicken and the sauce in a roasting pan and cook, uncovered, 45 to 50 minutes, or until tender, basting with sauce two or three times during cooking. Serve hot, garnished with twists of lime and lemon.

Makes 4 servings.

8 oz. chicken livers
2 tablespoons vegetable oil
2 onions, finely sliced
3 garlic cloves, crushed
2 teaspoons Garam Masala, page 51
½ teaspoon ground turmeric
Salt and pepper to taste
2 tablespoons lemon juice
2 tablespoons chopped fresh parsley
Parsley sprigs, to garnish

Rinse chicken livers and remove any green-tinged parts. Set aside.

Heat oil in a skillet, add onions and cook, stirring, over medium heat about 8 minutes, until soft and golden brown. Stir in garlic, Garam Masala, turmeric, salt and pepper. Cook 1 minute, then stir in chicken livers and fry about 5 minutes, stirring frequently, until livers are browned on outside, but still slightly pink in the center. Sprinkle with lemon juice and parsley. Serve hot, garnished with parsley sprigs.

Makes 4 appetizer servings.

NOTE: Frozen chicken livers can be used; thaw and drain before using.

SWEET SAFFRON RICE

1½ cups basmati rice
1 teaspoon saffron threads
3 tablespoons boiling water
3 tablespoons vegetable oil
6 whole cloves
6 green cardamom pods, bruised
1 (3-inch) cinnamon stick
½ cup raisins
3 tablespoons sugar
Salt to taste
Flat-leaf parsley sprigs

Place rice in a sieve and rinse under cold running water until water runs clear.

Put rice in a bowl with 2½ cups water and soak 30 minutes. Put saffron in a small bowl, add boiling water and soak. Heat oil in a heavy saucepan, add cloves, cardamom pods and cinnamon and cook 1 minute. Drain rice and reserve the soaking water. Add rice to the pan and cook 2 to 3 minutes until opaque and light golden.

Stir in reserved water, saffron and its soaking water, raisins, sugar and salt. Bring to a boil, then reduce heat and cover. Simmer 12 to 15 minutes, stirring once or twice until liquid is absorbed and rice is very tender. Remove spices before serving. Serve hot, garnished with parsley.

Makes 4 servings.

NOTE: The whole spices in the rice are not meant to be eaten.

FRAGRANT FRIED RICE

1¼ cups basmati rice
3 tablespoons vegetable oil
8 whole cloves
4 black cardamom pods, bruised
1 bay leaf
1 (3-inch) cinnamon stick
1 teaspoon black peppercorns
1 teaspoon cumin seeds
1 teaspoon coriander seeds
Salt to taste
1 small cauliflower, cut into tiny flowerets
1 onion, sliced into rings
Onion rings and bay leaves, to garnish

Place rice in a sieve and rinse under cold running water until water runs clear.

Put in a bowl with 2½ cups water and soak 30 minutes. Heat oil in a heavy saucepan, add cloves, cardamom pods, bay leaf, cinnamon, peppercorns, cumin seeds, coriander seeds and cook 1 minute. Add onion and cook 5 minutes, until softened. Drain rice and reserve the soaking water.

Add rice to the pan and cook 2 to 3 minutes until opaque and light golden. Stir in reserved water, salt and cauliflower. Bring to a boil, reduce heat and cover. Simmer 12 to 15 minutes, stirring once or twice, until liquid is absorbed and rice and cauliflower are tender. Remove whole spices before serving. Serve hot, garnished with onion rings and bay leaves.

Makes 4 servings.

NOTE: The whole spices in the rice are not meant to be eaten.

LENTIL-STUFFED PEPPERS

STUFFED OKRA

2/3 cup red split lentils
4 tablespoons vegetable oil
4 medium green or red bell peppers
1 teaspoon cumin seeds
2 onions, finely chopped
2 green chiles, seeded, chopped
1 (1-inch) piece fresh gingerroot, grated
1 tablespoon ground coriander
1¼ cups water
Salt and pepper to taste
2 tablespoons chopped cilantro (fresh coriander)
Cilantro leaves, to garnish

1 lb. small okra
2 tablespoons mango powder, see note below
1 tablespoon ground coriander
2 teaspoons ground cumin
¼ teaspoon red (cayenne) pepper
1 teaspoon Garam Masala, page 51
Salt to taste
2 tablespoons vegetable oil
1 onion, sliced
6 tomatoes, peeled
Lemon slices, to garnish

Rinse lentils, then soak in cold water 30 minutes.

Heat half the oil in a skillet. Add peppers and cook 3 to 5 minutes, until golden brown. Drain on paper towels; cool. Add remaining oil to pan, add cumin seeds; cook until just beginning to pop. Add onions and chiles and cook, stirring, 8 minutes, until onions are soft and golden brown. Stir in gingerroot and ground coriander. Drain lentils; add to pan with 1¼ cups water. Stir well, then cover.

Rinse okra and pat dry with paper towel. Trim off stems, then cut a slit along one side of each pod stopping ¼ inch from each end. Mix together mango powder, coriander, cumin, cayenne, Garam Masala and salt.

Pry open okra pods with your thumb and sprinkle a little of the spice mix inside each pod. Set aside.

Cook over low heat 15 to 20 minutes, until tender and liquid has evaporated. Stir in salt, pepper and cilantro. Preheat oven to 350F (175C). Cut tops from peppers and remove seeds. Stuff peppers with lentil mixture and replace tops. Stand in a baking dish. Bake 15 to 20 minutes until peppers are soft. Serve hot, garnished with cilantro leaves.

Makes 4 servings.

Heat oil in a large saucepan and add onion. Cook about 5 minutes until softened. Cut tomatoes into wedges, remove and discard seeds. Add tomatoes to pan and cook, stirring once or twice, 2 minutes. Add okra, cover and cook gently 10 to 15 minutes, stirring occasionally until tender. Serve hot, garnished with lemon slices.

Makes 4 servings.

NOTE: Mango powder is available from Asian shops. where it is often called *amchoor* powder.

EGGPLANT TAHINI PÂTÉ

1 large eggplant
1 large clove garlic
3 shallots
½ to 1 teaspoon Garam Masala, page 51
3 tablespoons tahini (creamed sesame)
Finely grated peel 1 lemon
3 tablespoons lemon juice
Salt to taste
2 teaspoons olive oil
Cayenne pepper
Lemon slices, if desired, cut in half
Fresh parsley sprig, if desired
Pita bread, cut in strips

Preheat oven to 350F (175C). Prick egg-plant several times with a fork.

Bake eggplant in preheated oven 30 to 40 minutes or until softened and skin has turned dark brown. Cool, trim ends and peel eggplant. Process flesh in a blender or food processor with garlic, shallots, Garam Masala, tahini, lemon peel and juice until smooth and evenly combined.

Season with salt. Spoon mixture into a serving bowl, drizzle with olive oil and sprinkle with cayenne pepper. Garnish with lemon slices and parsley sprig, if desired, and serve with pita bread.

Makes 4 to 6 servings.

CARROTS WITH FRESH DILL

1 lb. carrots
1 tablespoon vegetable oil
2 tablespoons butter
¾ teaspoon cumin seeds
Pinch ground asafetida
1 (½-inch) piece fresh gingerroot, finely chopped
2 green chiles, seeded, finely sliced
1 teaspoon ground coriander
¼ teaspoon ground turmeric
6 tablespoons water
4 tablespoons chopped fresh dill
Salt to taste
Dill sprigs, to garnish

Cut carrots into ⅛ x 1-inch strips. Set aside. Heat oil and butter in a heavy saucepan and cook cumin seeds about 30 seconds, until they begin to pop. Add asafetida, ginger-root, chiles, coriander and turmeric; cook 2 minutes. Stir in carrots and water.

Cover and cook over medium heat 5 min-utes, or until carrots are just tender. Uncover, add chopped dill and salt, increase heat and cook over high heat about 2 minutes to evaporate any excess liquid. Serve hot, garnished with dill sprigs.

Makes 4 servings.

NOTE: This recipe is also delicious chilled and served as a salad.

MIXED VEGETABLE CURRY —

3 tablespoons vegetable oil
1 onion, sliced
1 teaspoon ground cumin
1 teaspoon chile powder
2 teaspoons ground coriander
1 teaspoon ground turmeric
8 ounces potatoes, diced
6 ounces cauliflower, broken into flowerets
4 ounces green beans, sliced
6 ounces carrots, diced
4 tomatoes, peeled, chopped
1¼ cups hot vegetable stock
Onion rings, to garnish

Heat oil in a large saucepan, add onion and cook 5 minutes until softened. Stir in cumin, chile powder, coriander and turmeric; cook 2 minutes. Add potatoes, cauliflower, green beans and carrots, tossing them in the spices until coated.

Add tomatoes and stock and cover. Bring to a boil, then reduce heat and simmer 10 to 12 minutes or until vegetables are just tender. Serve hot, garnished with onion rings.

Makes 4 servings.

VARIATION: Use any mixture of vegetables to make a total of 1-½ pounds — turnips, zucchini, eggplant, parsnips and leeks are all suitable.

SPICED BROWN LENTILS —

1¼ cups whole brown lentils
1¼ cups Coconut Milk, page 51
¼ teaspoon chile powder
½ teaspoon ground turmeric
2 tablespoons vegetable oil
1 onion, finely chopped
4 curry leaves, optional
½ stalk lemon grass
1 (3-inch) cinnamon stick
Lemon thyme sprigs, to garnish

Rinse lentils, put in a bowl, cover with cold water and leave to soak 6 hours or overnight.

Drain lentils and put them in a large saucepan with Coconut Milk, chile powder and turmeric. Bring to a boil, cover and simmer 30 minutes, or until just tender. Heat oil in a separate pan, add onion, curry leaves, lemon grass and cinnamon and fry, stirring, over a medium heat 8 minutes, or until onion is soft and golden brown.

Stir into lentil mixture and simmer another 10 minutes, or until liquid has evaporated and lentils are soft but not broken up. Remove whole spices and serve hot, garnished with thyme sprigs.

Makes 4 servings.

NOTE: Substitute a few sprigs of lemon thyme if lemon grass is unavailable.

—CURRIED GARBANZO BEANS—

1 cup dried garbanzo beans
Salt to taste
2 tablespoons vegetable oil
1 small onion, finely chopped
1 (1-inch) piece fresh gingerroot, grated
2 garlic cloves, crushed
½ teaspoon ground turmeric
1 teaspoon ground cumin
1 teaspoon Garam Masala, page 51
½ teaspoon chile powder
2 tablespoons chopped cilantro (fresh coriander)

Rinse garbanzo, put them in a bowl, cover with cold water and soak overnight.

Drain beans, add 2 cups cold water and salt. Boil 10 minutes, then reduce heat and simmer, partially covered 1 hour. In a separate pan, heat oil, add onion; cook about 8 minutes, until soft and golden brown.

Add gingerroot, garlic, turmeric, cumin, Garam Masala and chile powder; cook 1 minute. Stir in beans and their cooking water and bring to a boil. Cover and simmer 20 minutes, until beans are very tender, but still whole. Serve hot, sprinkled with chopped cilantro.

Makes 4 servings.

— TAMIL NADU VEGETABLES—

⅔ cup red split lentils
½ teaspoon ground turmeric
2½ cups water
1 small eggplant
¼ cup vegetable oil
⅓ cup shredded coconut
1 teaspoon cumin seeds
½ teaspoon mustard seeds
2 dried red chiles, crushed
1 red bell pepper, seeded, sliced
4 ounces zucchini, thickly sliced
3 ounces green beans, cut into ¾-inch pieces
⅔ cup vegetable stock
Salt to taste
Red bell pepper strips, to garnish

Rinse lentils and put in a large pan with turmeric and water. Boil 10 minutes, then reduce heat and cover.

Simmer 15 to 20 minutes until lentils are soft. Meanwhile, cut eggplant into ½-inch cubes. Heat oil in a large shallow pan, add coconut, cumin seeds, mustard seeds and chiles.

Cook 1 minute, then add eggplant, bell pepper, zucchini, green beans, stock and salt. Bring to a boil, reduce heat, cover and simmer 10 to 15 minutes, until vegetables are just tender. Stir in lentils and any cooking liquid and cook another 5 minutes. Serve hot, garnished with bell pepper strips.

Makes 4 servings.

MUSHROOM CURRY

SPINACH & BEAN DUMPLINGS

1 pound button mushrooms
2 green chiles, seeded
2 teaspoons ground coriander
1 teaspoon ground cumin
½ teaspoon chile powder
2 garlic cloves, crushed
1 onion, cut into wedges
⅔ cup Coconut Milk, page 51
Salt to taste
2 tablespoons butter
Fresh bay leaves, to garnish, if desired

Wipe mushrooms and trim stalks. Set aside.

Put chiles, coriander, cumin, chile powder, garlic, onion and Coconut Milk in a blender or food processor fitted with the metal blade and blend until smooth. Season to taste with salt.

Melt butter in a saucepan, add mushrooms and cook 3 to 4 minutes until golden brown. Add spice mixture, reduce heat and simmer, uncovered, 10 minutes, or until mushrooms are tender. Serve hot, garnished with bay leaves, if desired.

Makes 4 servings.

1 cup yellow split mung beans
2 ounces frozen chopped spinach, thawed
2 tablespoons chopped cilantro (fresh coriander)
2 green chiles, seeded, chopped
Large pinch baking powder
½ teaspoon salt
Vegetable oil for deep-frying
Chile flowers, to garnish

Put beans in a bowl, cover them in water and soak 4 hours. Drain and rinse under cold running water.

Put beans in a blender or food processor fitted with the metal blade and process, until smooth, light and fluffy, scraping mixture from sides of bowl several times. Press excess water from spinach and mix into the ground beans. Stir in cilantro, chiles, baking powder and salt.

Half-fill a deep pan or deep-fryer with oil and heat to 375F (190C) or until a 1-inch bread cube browns in 50 seconds. Drop 6 level tablespoons of mixture into the hot oil; fry 4 to 5 minutes, or until golden brown. Drain dumplings on paper towel and keep warm while cooking remaining mixture. Serve hot, garnished with chile flowers.

Makes 4 servings.

CHEESY STUFFED TOMATOES

8 tomatoes
2 tablespoons vegetable oil
1 small onion, finely chopped
1 garlic clove, crushed
1 (1-inch) piece fresh gingerroot, grated
1 teaspoon ground cumin
½ teaspoon ground turmeric
½ teaspoon red (cayenne) pepper
2 teaspoons ground coriander
Salt to taste
½ cup fresh farmers cheese
¼ cup shredded Cheddar cheese
1 tablespoon chopped cilantro (fresh coriander)

Cut a slice from the top of each tomato. Scoop out centers, discard seeds, then chop pulp and reserve. Turn tomatoes upside down on paper towels and drain.

Heat oil in a small skillet, add onion and cook 5 minutes or until soft, stirring occasionally. Stir in garlic and gingerroot and cook 1 minute. Stir in cumin, turmeric, cayenne, coriander and salt; cook 1 minute more.

Stir in tomato pulp and cook, uncovered, about 5 minutes, until thick. Preheat oven to 375F (190C). Stir farmers cheese and half the Cheddar cheese into spice mixture and spoon into tomato shells. Sprinkle remaining Cheddar cheese on top and place in a baking pan. Bake 10 to 15 minutes, until tops are golden brown and tomatoes are soft. Sprinkle with chopped cilantro and serve hot.

Makes 4 servings.

ONION BHAJIS

¾ cup garbanzo bean flour, sifted
1 tablespoon vegetable oil plus extra for deep-frying
1 teaspoon ground coriander
1 teaspoon ground cumin
Salt to taste
2 green chiles, seeded, finely chopped
½ cup warm water
2 onions, finely sliced
Cilantro (fresh coriander) leaves, to garnish

Put flour in a blender or food processor fitted with the metal blade. Add 1 tablespoon oil, coriander, cumin, salt, chiles and water. Process until blended and smooth. Pour batter into a bowl, cover and let stand in a warm place 30 minutes.

Stir in onions. Half-fill a deep pan or deep-fryer with oil and heat over medium heat to 375F (190C) or until a 1-inch bread cube browns in 50 seconds. Add mixture in 2 tablespoon amounts to oil in batches; fry 5 to 6 minutes until golden. Do not cook too quickly or the centers will not cook completely. Drain on paper towels. Serve hot, garnished with cilantro leaves.

Makes 4 servings.

SPICY OKRA

PEPPERY MOZARELLA SALAD

12 ounces okra
2 tablespoons vegetable oil
1 (1-inch) piece fresh gingerroot, grated
1 teaspoon ground turmeric
½ teaspoon chile powder
Salt to taste
1 teaspoon garbanzo bean flour
3 tablespoons water
1¼ cups plain yogurt
2 tablespoons chopped cilantro (fresh coriander),
    to garnish

6 ounces Mozzarella cheese
2 large beefsteak tomatoes, cut in half
1 ripe avocado
2 shallots, peeled, thinly sliced
⅓ cup olive oil
2 tablespoons lemon juice
½ teaspoon sugar
Salt to taste
¼ to ½ teaspoon dry mustard
1 to 2 teaspoons green peppercorns, crushed
½ teaspoon dried oregano
Crusty bread or bread sticks

Thinly slice cheese and tomato and arrange
on 4 small plates.

Rinse okra and pat dry with paper towels,
then cut into thick slices. Heat oil in a
medium saucepan, add okra and cook 4
minutes, stirring occasionally. Stir in gingerroot, turmeric, chile powder, salt and flour;
cook 1 minute more.

Cut avocado in thin slices and arrange with
cheese and tomato. Separate shallots in
rings and scatter over salad.

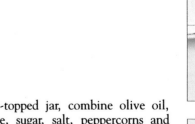

Stir in water, then cover and simmer 10
minutes, or until okra is tender. Stir in
yogurt and reheat gently. Serve hot,
sprinkled with cilantro.

Makes 4 servings.

NOTE: Choose okra pods that are about 4
inches long – larger pods are tough and
stringy to eat.

In a screw-topped jar, combine olive oil,
lemon juice, sugar, salt, peppercorns and
oregano. Shake vigorously until well
blended. Spoon over salad and let marinate
1 hour. Garnish with basil, if desired, and
serve with warm crusty bread or bread sticks.

Makes 4 servings.

FISH IN A PACKAGE

4 (6 to 8 oz.) fish steaks, such as sea bass, cod
   or salmon
1 or 2 fresh or frozen banana leaves, optional
Salt and pepper to taste
1¼ cups finely grated fresh coconut
2 ounces fresh mint, chopped
4 garlic cloves, crushed
1 teaspoon ground cumin
4 green chiles, seeded, chopped
2 tablespoons lemon juice
¼ cup cider vinegar
1 tablespoon vegetable oil
¾ cup water
8 dried curry leaves, optional
Mint leaves and lemon slices, to garnish

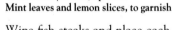

Wipe fish steaks and place each in center of
a 12-inch square of banana leaf or foil.
Sprinkle fish with salt and pepper. Mix
together coconut, mint, garlic, cumin,
chiles and lemon juice in a medium bowl.
Spoon a quarter of mixture on each fish
steak. Fold sides of banana leaf or foil over to
seal completely. Tie banana leaf parcels with
fine string, if necessary.

Pour vinegar, oil and water into the bottom
of a large steamer, add curry leaves and bring
to a boil. Place fish package over boiling
liquid. Steam 12 to 15 minutes, or until fish
just begins to flake. Open packages and
serve, garnished with mint and lemon slices.

Makes 4 servings.

HOT MUSSELS WITH CUMIN

3 pounds mussels
2 tablespoons vegetable oil
1 large onion, finely chopped
1 (1-inch) piece fresh gingerroot, grated
6 garlic cloves, crushed
2 green chiles, seeded, finely chopped
½ teaspoon ground turmeric
2 teaspoons ground cumin
1 cup water
1¾ cups shredded fresh coconut
2 tablespoons chopped cilantro (fresh coriander)
Cilantro (fresh coriander) leaves, to garnish

Scrub mussels clean in several changes of
fresh cold water and pull off beards.

Discard any mussels that are cracked or do
not closely tightly when tapped. Set other
mussels aside. Heat oil in a large saucepan
and add onion. Cook, stirring, 5 minutes
until soft, then add gingerroot, garlic,
chiles, turmeric and cumin. Cook 2 minutes, stirring constantly.

Add mussels, coconut and water; bring to a
boil. Cover and cook over high heat,
shaking pan frequently, about 5 minutes or
until mussels have opened. Discard any that
remain closed. Spoon mussels into a serving
dish, pour cooking liquid over mussels and
sprinkle with chopped cilantro. Garnish
with cilantro leaves and serve at once.

Makes 4 servings.

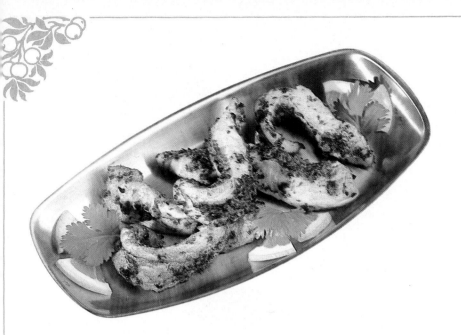

CILANTRO & CHILE FISH

1¾ lbs. white fish fillets, such as monkfish or sole
1 tablespoon plus 1 teaspoon lemon juice
Salt and pepper to taste
3 ounces cilantro (fresh coriander) leaves
4 green chiles, seeded, chopped
3 garlic cloves, crushed
1 to 2 tablespoons water
1 cup plain yogurt
Vegetable oil for deep-frying
Lemon wedges and cilantro (fresh coriander) leaves,
  to garnish

Trim any skin and bones from fish. Cut flesh into 1- x 3-inch strips

Spread fish strips in a shallow non-metal dish and sprinkle with lemon juice, salt and pepper. Set aside. Put cilantro, chiles, garlic and water in a blender or food processor fitted with the metal blade and process until smooth, frequently scraping down mixture. Squeeze out excess liquid from paste, place in a shallow dish and stir in yogurt.

Heat oil in a deep pan or deep-fryer to 350F (175C) or until a 1-inch bread cube browns in 65 seconds. Drain fish and pat dry with paper towels. Dip the strips in yogurt mixture, coating them all over and fry a few at a time 2 to 3 minutes, until golden brown. Drain on paper towels, then serve at once, garnished with lemon wedges and cilantro leaves.

Makes 4 servings.

SOLE WITH DILL STUFFING

4 (6-oz.) sole fillets, skinned
1 tablespoon lemon juice
Salt and pepper to taste
1½ tablespoons vegetable oil
1 garlic clove, crushed
1 (1-inch) piece fresh gingerroot, grated
¼ teaspoon red (cayenne) pepper
¼ teaspoon ground turmeric
4 green onions, finely chopped
8 tablespoons finely chopped fresh dill
¼ cup water
Dill sprigs, to garnish

Rinse fish fillets and pat dry with paper towels.

Lay fillets skinned side up on a work surface and sprinkle with lemon juice, salt and pepper. Set aside. Preheat oven to 350F (175C). Heat oil in a skillet. Add garlic, gingerroot, cayenne, turmeric and green onions. Cook over low heat 3 minutes or until onions are soft and golden, stirring occasionally. Remove from heat, cool, then stir in chopped dill.

Divide stuffing among fillets and spread evenly over fish. Roll fillets up from thickest end. Grease a shallow ovenproof dish. Arrange fish rolls, seam side down in the dish; add water. Cover with foil and bake 15 to 20 minutes, or until fish just begins to flake. Serve hot, topped with cooking juices and garnished with dill sprigs.

Makes 4 servings

SPICY GARLIC FISH FRY

SPICY SHRIMP PATTIES

1½ lbs. mixed white fish fillets, such as sole, whiting, cod or monkfish
1 teaspoon ground cumin
½ teaspoon ground coriander
1 teaspoon ground anise seeds
½ teaspoon chile powder
3 garlic cloves, crushed
1 tablespoon lemon juice
Salt to taste
Vegetable oil for deep-frying
Lettuce leaves and sliced radishes, to garnish

Remove any skin and bones from fish, rinse and pat dry with paper towels. Cut into large chunks.

Mix together cumin, coriander, ground anise, chile powder, garlic, lemon juice and salt, blending to a smooth paste. Spread over fish, cover and refrigerate 1 hour.

Half-fill a deep pan or deep-fryer with oil and heat to 350F (175C) or until a 1-inch bread cube browns in 50 seconds. Cook fish, a few pieces at a time, 2 to 3 minutes, until golden brown. Drain on paper towels. Serve hot, garnished with lettuce and radish slices.

Makes 4 servings.

12 ounces white fish fillets, such as sole, cod or whiting
6 ounces cooked peeled shrimp, chopped
4 green onions, chopped
1 (1-inch) piece fresh gingerroot, grated
2 tablespoons chopped cilantro (fresh coriander)
1 tablespoon chopped fresh mint
2 cups fresh white bread crumbs
Salt and red (cayenne) pepper to taste
1 egg yolk, beaten
2 tablespoons lemon juice
¾ cup garbanzo bean flour
1 tablespoon ground coriander
½ cup water
¼ cup vegetable oil
Mint sprigs and lemon slices, to garnish

Remove any skin and bones from fish, rinse and pat dry with paper towels. Mince fish, then transfer to a bowl. Stir in shrimp, green onions, gingerroot, cilantro, mint, ½ cup of breadcrumbs, salt and cayenne. Add egg yolk and lemon juice; mix well. Divide mixture into 16 equal portions and form into ½-inch-thick rounds. Roll patties in remaining bread crumbs to coat completely.

Put flour, coriander, salt and cayenne in a small bowl, add water and mix to a smooth batter. Heat oil in a skillet. Dip patties in batter; fry 2 to 3 minutes on each side until golden brown. Drain on paper towels and serve hot, garnished with mint and lemon slices.

Makes 4 servings.

FISH IN HOT SAUCE

4 (8-oz. each) whole fish, such as mackerel or
trout, cleaned
4 dill sprigs
4 lime slices
4 tablespoons vegetable oil
4 green onions, sliced
1 (½-inch) piece fresh gingerroot, grated
1 garlic clove, crushed
1 teaspoon mustard seeds
¼ teaspoon red (cayenne) pepper
1 tablespoon tamarind paste
2 tablespoons tomato paste
6 tablespoons water
Dill sprigs and lime slices, to garnish

Rinse fish and pat dry with paper towels.
Slash two or three times on each side with a
sharp knife and tuck a sprig of dill and a lime
slice inside each fish. Set aside. Heat 2
tablespoons of the oil in a small saucepan.
Add onions and cook, stirring, 2 to 3 minutes, until softened. Add gingerroot, garlic
and mustard seeds; cook 1 minute more.

Stir in cayenne, tamarind paste, tomato
paste and water. Bring to a boil, reduce heat
and simmer, uncovered, about 5 minutes,
until thickened slightly. Meanwhile, heat
grill. Place fish on grill rack, brush with
remaining oil and cook about 5 minutes on
each side, until fish just begins to flake,
basting occasionally with oil. Serve hot with
the sauce. Garnish with dill and lime slices.

Makes 4 servings.

STEAMED FISH & VEGETABLES

4 (8-oz. each) whole red mullet, red snapper or sea
bream, cleaned
1 tablespoon plus 1 teaspoon Garam Masala, page 51
½ teaspoon ground turmeric
2 tablespoons chopped cilantro (fresh coriander)
1 tablespoon chopped fresh parsley
1 (1-inch) piece fresh gingerroot, grated
4 lemon slices
2 tablespoons vegetable oil
8 new potatoes, sliced
3 carrots, sliced
4 zucchini, sliced
Salt and pepper to taste
Parsley sprigs, to garnish

Rinse fish and pat dry with paper towels.
Slash three times on each side. Mix together
Garam Masala, turmeric, cilantro, parsley
and gingerroot. Rub into flesh and skin of
fish. Tuck a slice of lemon inside each fish
and set aside. Heat oil in a skillet, add
potatoes and carrots and cook, stirring
frequently, 5 to 6 minutes, until slightly
softened and beginning to brown.

Add zucchini to pan and cook 1 minute
more. Season with salt and pepper. Using a
slotted spoon, transfer vegetables to a
steamer. Lay fish on top. Cover and steam
20 to 25 minutes, or until fish just starts to
flake and vegetables are tender. Serve at
once, garnished with parsley.

Makes 4 servings.

SHRIMP & FISH BALL CURRY

CREAMY SAFFRON FISH CURRY

1 pound white fish fillets, such as sole, cod, whiting or monkfish, skinned
4 ounces cooked peeled shrimp
1½ cups fresh white bread crumbs
2 eggs, beaten separately
2 tablespoons chopped cilantro (fresh coriander)
2 teaspoons lemon juice
Salt and pepper to taste
2 tablespoons vegetable oil plus extra for deep-frying
1 large onion, finely chopped
2 green chiles, seeded, chopped
4 garlic cloves, crushed
½ teaspoon ground turmeric
⅔ cup Coconut Milk, page 51
1 (14-oz.) can chopped tomatoes

1½ pounds white fish fillets, such as sole, whiting or cod
Pinch of saffron threads
2 tablespoons boiling water
3 tablespoons vegetable oil
2 onions, chopped
3 garlic cloves, crushed
1 (1-inch) piece fresh gingerroot, grated
1 teaspoon ground turmeric
1 tablespoon ground coriander
2 tablespoons Garam Masala, page 51
Salt and red (cayenne) pepper to taste
2 teaspoons garbanzo bean flour
1 cup plain yogurt
¼ cup whipping cream
Shreds of lemon peel and red bell pepper, to garnish

Rinse fish and remove any bones. Mince fish and shrimp, then transfer to a large bowl. Stir in 1 cup of bread crumbs, 1 egg, cilantro, lemon juice, salt and pepper. Mix well and form into 24 balls. Roll balls in remaining egg, then in remaining bread crumbs to coat completely. Cover and refrigerate 30 minutes, Meanwhile, heat 2 tablespoons oil in a heavy saucepan, add onion and cook, stirring, 5 minutes to soften.

Rinse fish, remove any skin and bones and pat dry with paper towels. Cut into large chunks and set aside. Put saffron in a small bowl with boiling water; let soak. Heat oil in a large shallow pan, add onions and cook, stirring, about 5 minutes, until soft, but not brown.

Add chiles, garlic and turmeric; cook 2 minutes more. Stir in Coconut Milk and tomatoes and cook, uncovered 20 minutes, until reduced and thickened, stirring occasionally. Half-fill a deep pan or deep-fryer with oil and heat to 375F (190C), or until a 1-inch bread cube browns in 50 seconds. Fry fish balls 3 to 5 minutes, until golden brown. Drain on paper towels and serve with the sauce.

Makes 4 servings.

Add garlic, gingerroot, turmeric, coriander, Garam Masala, salt and cayenne; cook 1 minute more. Stir in flour; cook 1 minute, then remove from heat. Stir in yogurt and cream; bring slowly to a boil. Add fish. Reduce heat, cover and simmer gently 10 to 15 minutes, until fish just begins to flake. Serve hot, garnished with lemon peel and bell pepper.

Makes 4 servings.

SCANDINAVIAN FISH SALAD

GRILLED SPICED FISH

⅔ cup malt vinegar
⅔ cup water
3 tablespoons sugar
1 tablespoon Pickling Spice
4 fresh herrings, cleaned, filleted
1-¼ cups sour cream
3 tablespoons mayonnaise
2 teaspoons Dijon-style mustard
1 onion, halved, thinly sliced
1 green delicious apple
1 red delicious apple
Red leaf lettuce leaves, if desired
4 green onion daisies, if desired
Fresh dill sprigs, if desired

In a small saucepan, combine vinegar and water. Add sugar and pickling spice.

Bring to a boil, stirring to dissolve sugar. Boil 2 minutes; cool. Strain and discard spices. Cut herring fillets in ½-inch-wide strips and place in a shallow dish. Pour cold marinade over fish. Cover and marinate several hours or overnight.

Drain herring strips. In a bowl, combine sour cream, mayonnaise, mustard and onion. Cut apples in fourths, remove cores and slice thinly (do not peel). Add sliced apples and herrings to sour cream mixture and mix together gently until coated with dressing. Arrange lettuce leaves on 4 plates. Spoon herring mixture on plates and garnish with green onion daisies and dill sprigs, if desired. Serve chilled.

Makes 4 servings.

4 (8-oz) sole, skinned
Salt and pepper to taste
⅔ cup plain yogurt
2 garlic cloves, crushed
2 teaspoons Garam Masala, page 51
1 teaspoon ground coriander
½ teaspoon chile powder
1 tablespoon lemon juice
Lemon wedges, to garnish

Rinse fish, pat dry with paper towels and place in a shallow non-metal dish. Sprinkle with salt and pepper.

Mix together yogurt, garlic, Garam Masala, coriander, chile powder and lemon juice. Pour over fish. Cover and refrigerate 2 to 3 hours to allow fish to absorb flavours.

Preheat broiler. Transfer fish to a broiler rack; cook about 8 minutes, until fish just begins to flake, basting with cooking juices and turning over halfway through cooking. Serve hot, garnished with lemon wedges.

Makes 4 servings.

CARROT HALVA

1-¼ lbs. carrots, coarsely grated
3 cups milk
8 green cardamom pods, bruised
¼ cup vegetable oil
¼ cup superfine sugar
2 tablespoons raisins
⅓ cup shelled pistachios, coarsely chopped
1 cup thick plain yogurt, to serve

Put carrots, milk and cardamom pods in a heavy saucepan; bring to a boil over high heat.

Reduce heat to medium and cook, uncovered, about 50 minutes, until liquid has been absorbed, stirring occasionally. Remove cardamom pods. Heat oil in a large skillet, add carrot mixture and cook, stirring constantly, 10 to 15 minutes, until mixture turns a deep red color.

Stir in sugar, raisins and half the pistachios. Cook 1 to 2 minutes more to heat through. Serve warm, topped with yogurt and sprinkled with remaining pistachios.

Makes 6 to 8 servings.

PISTACHIO HALVA

1-¼ cups shelled pistachios
1 cup boiling water
2 tablespoons milk
½ cup sugar
1-½ tablespoons butter or ghee
1 teaspoon vanilla extract

Put pistachios in a bowl, top with boiling water and soak 30 minutes. Grease and line an 8-inch square pan with waxed paper.

Drain pistachios thoroughly and put in a blender or food processor fitted with the metal blade. Add milk and process until finely chopped, scraping mixture down from sides once or twice. Stir in sugar. Heat a large non-stick skillet, add butter and melt over medium-low heat. Add nut paste and cook about 15 minutes, stirring constantly, until mixture is very thick.

Stir in vanilla extract, then spoon into prepared pan and spread evenly. Cool completely, then cut into 20 squares using a sharp knife.

Makes about 20 squares.

NOTE: This halva will keep 2 to 3 weeks, covered and stored in the refrigerator.

SAFFRON YOGURT

2-½ cups plain yogurt
Pinch of saffron threads
2 tablespoons boiling water
Seeds from 6 cardamom pods
3 tablespoons superfine sugar
Lemon peel and cardamom seeds, to decorate

Pour yogurt into a nylon sieve lined with cheesecloth and refrigerate to drain overnight.

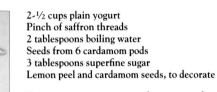

Put saffron and boiling water in a small bowl and soak 30 minutes. Turn drained yogurt into a bowl and stir in saffron and its soaking liquid.

Put cardamom seeds in a mortar and crush lightly with a pestle. Stir into yogurt with sugar. Serve chilled, decorated with lemon peel and cardamom seeds.

Makes 4 to 6 servings.

ICED COFFEE CREAM

2 tablespoons instant coffee
4 teaspoons light-brown sugar
⅓ cup boiling water
¼ teaspoon ground cinnamon
Few pinches mixed spice
⅔ cup cold water
1-½ cups chilled milk
1 teaspoon vanilla extract
5 tablespoons whipping cream
8 ice cubes
4 small scoops vanilla ice cream
½ teaspoon sweetened cocoa powder
4 (3-inch) cinnamon sticks
Lime slices, if desired
Grated chocolate, if desired

Dissolve coffee and brown sugar in boiling water. Add cinnamon and mixed spice.

Add cold water and stir well. Add milk, vanilla and whipping cream. Whisk lightly until evenly combined.

Put 2 ice cubes into each glass. Half fill with coffee mixture. Add a scoop of ice cream to each glass and top up with remaining coffee. Sprinkle with unsweetened cocoa powder. Garnish with cinnamon sticks, lime slices and grated chocolate, if desired. Serve at once with long-handled spoons.

Makes 4 servings.

Variation: For a sweeter version, increase brown sugar to taste. If desired, top each with a little whipped cream.

SAFFRON RICE PUDDING

COCONUT PANCAKES

1-¼ cups basmati rice
2-½ cups water
⅓ cup milk
Pinch of saffron threads
2 tablespoons butter
2 green cardamom pods, bruised
1 (1-inch) cinnamon stick
2 cloves
½ cup raisins
¼ cup sugar
⅓ cup sliced almonds, toasted

Wash rice under cold running water and put into a large saucepan with water.

Bring to a boil, reduce heat and simmer 5 minutes, then drain. Measure 2 tablespoons of milk into a small bowl, add saffron and soak 5 minutes. Heat butter in a heavy saucepan, add rice, cardamom pods, cinnamon and cloves and cook 2 to 3 minutes, or until rice becomes opaque.

Stir in remaining milk, saffron milk, raisins and sugar and bring to a boil. Cover and simmer about 6 to 8 minutes, until rice is tender and liquid has been absorbed. Remove whole spices and serve hot, with almonds scattered on top.

Makes 4 servings.

1 cup all-purpose flour
Pinch of salt
1 egg, beaten
1-¼ cups milk
3 tablespoons brown sugar
3 cups shredded fresh coconut
1 (½-inch) piece fresh gingerroot, grated
6 anise seeds, crushed
Plain yogurt, to serve
⅓ cup shredded fresh coconut, to serve

Sift together flour and salt into a medium bowl. Whisk in egg and half of the milk to make a smooth, thick batter.

Set batter aside in a cool place 30 minutes, then stir in enough of remaining milk to make batter the consistency of light cream. Heat a 6-inch skillet over medium-high heat, brush with a little oil and pour in 2 to 3 tablespoons batter, tipping pan to coat bottom. Cook 1 to 2 minutes until browned, then flip pancake over and cook other side for about 30 seconds, until browned.

Turn pancake onto a plate and make about 7 more pancakes in same way, stacking them on the plate as they are ready. In a small bowl, mix together sugar, coconut, gingerroot and anise seeds. Spread a spoonful of mixture on each pancake and fold into quarters. Cover and refrigerate about 30 minutes. Serve cold with yogurt and coconut.

Makes 4 servings.

GOLDEN SEMOLINA PUDDING

INDIAN FRUIT SALAD

½ cup sugar
⅔ cup water
3 tablespoons butter or ghee
¾ cup semolina
Seeds from 3 cardamom pods
¼ cup raisins
½ cup sliced almonds, toasted

Put sugar and water in a heavy saucepan. Cook over low heat, stirring occasionally, until sugar has dissolved. Increase heat and bring to a boil and boil 1 minute. Remove from heat and set aside.

Melt butter in a large heavy skillet, add semolina and cook 8 to 10 minutes over medium heat, stirring constantly, until semolina turns golden brown.

Remove from heat and cool slightly, then stir in sugar syrup and cardamom seeds. Cook over low heat 3 to 5 minutes until thick, stirring frequently. Stir in half the raisins and almonds. Serve warm, decorated with remaining raisins and almonds.

Makes 4 to 6 servings.

2 mangoes
2 bananas
2 oranges
2 ounces black grapes
2 ounces green grapes
1 papaya
Grated peel and juice of 1 lime
¼ cup superfine sugar
Freshly ground black pepper to taste
Plain yogurt, to serve

Peel and seed mangoes and cut flesh into thin slices, reserving any scraps. Peel and diagonally slice bananas.

Peel and section oranges, working over a bowl to catch juice. Halve and seed both black and green grapes. Peel and halve papaya, scoop out seeds and cut flesh into slices, reserving any scraps. Put fruit in a serving bowl and stir to combine. Put orange juice, lime juice, sugar and scraps of mango and papaya in blender or food processor fitted with the metal blade and process until smooth. Add lime peel and pepper. Pour over fruit and chill at least 1 hour before serving with yogurt.

Makes 4 to 6 servings.

NOTE: Substitute other fruits, such as melon, guava or pineapple, if preferred.

TOASTED ALMOND TOFFEE

2 cups sugar
1 cup water
2 cups nonfat dry milk powder
1 teaspoon vanilla extract
¼ cup flaked almonds, toasted

Grease and line an 8-inch square pan with waxed paper. Put sugar and water in a large heavy saucepan. Heat gently, stirring occasionally, until sugar is dissolved.

Increase heat and bring to a boil, and boil over medium-high heat until a few drops of mixture will form a soft ball in cold water. Stir in milk powder and cook 3 to 4 minutes more, stirring all the time, until mixture begins to dry on spoon. Stir in vanilla.

Pour into prepared pan and spread evenly. Scatter almonds over top and press into surface. Leave to cool slightly, then cut into 25 squares with a sharp knife while still warm. Leave in pan until cold and firm.

Makes 25 squares.

COCONUT LAYER CAKE

½ cup all-purpose flour
1-⅔ cups Coconut Milk, page 51
6 egg yolks, beaten
½ cup sugar
Seeds from 4 green cardamom pods, crushed
Pinch of freshly grated nutmeg
½ cup butter, melted
Plain yogurt and sliced bananas, to serve

Put flour in a medium bowl, whisk in coconut milk, egg yolks, sugar, cardamom seeds and nutmeg, then let batter stand 30 minutes.

Preheat oven to 425F (220C). Butter a 6-inch soufflé dish. Add 1 tablespoon butter to dish and heat in oven 5 minutes. Pour in 6 tablespoons of batter and bake 10 to 15 minutes, until firm to the touch and lightly browned. Brush with butter. Continue adding another three layers, brushing each cooked layer with butter before adding batter. Bake each layer 10 to 15 minutes.

Put soufflé dish in a baking pan half-filled with boiling water, then continue adding another three layers in same way as before. When last layer is cooked, remove dish from oven and cool. Run a knife around edge of dish to loosen cake and turn out onto a serving plate. Serve warm, with yogurt and sliced bananas.

Makes 4 to 6 servings.

APRICOT DESSERT

CASHEW NUT FUDGE

1-¾ cups dried apricots
1 cup water
1 cup superfine sugar
2 cups water
½ pint (1 cup) whipping cream
⅓ cup blanched almonds, chopped, toasted

Put apricots and 1 cup water in a medium saucepan; bring to a boil. Reduce heat, cover and simmer about 25 minutes, or until very soft.

Meanwhile, put sugar and 2 cups water in a heavy saucepan and heat gently, stirring occasionally, until sugar has dissolved. Increase heat, bring to a boil and boil 3 minutes, or until syrupy. Drain apricots and puree in a blender or food processor fitted with the metal blade. Add syrup and process again.

Pour into a bowl and cool, then refrigerate at least 1 hour. Whip cream until soft peaks form, fold half into apricot puree, leaving it slightly marbled, and spoon into serving dishes. Chill 30 minutes, then top with remaining cream and scatter with chopped almonds.

Makes 4 to 6 servings.

1-½ cups unsalted cashew nuts
1-½ cups boiling water
2 tablespoons milk
⅔ cup sugar
1 tablespoon butter or ghee
1 teaspoon vanilla extract
Few sheets of silver leaf

Put cashew nuts in a bowl, top with boiling water and soak 1 hour. Grease and line an 8-inch square pan with waxed paper.

Drain cashew nuts thoroughly and put in a blender or food processor fitted with the metal blade. Add milk and process until smooth, scraping mixture down from side once or twice. Stir in sugar. Heat a large non-stick skillet, add butter and melt over medium-low heat. Add nut paste and cook about 20 minutes, stirring constantly, until mixture is very thick.

Stir in vanilla extract, then spoon into prepared pan and spread evenly. Cool completely, then press silver leaf onto surface. Cut fudge into about 25 diamond shapes using a wet sharp knife.

Makes about 25 pieces.

NOTE: This fudge will keep for two to three weeks if stored in an airtight container.

FRESH MANGO CHUTNEY

2 mangoes
1 red chile, seeded, finely sliced
¼ cup chopped cashew nuts
¼ cup raisins
2 tablespoons chopped fresh mint
Pinch of asafetida
½ teaspoon ground cumin
¼ teaspoon red (cayenne) pepper
½ teaspoon ground coriander
Mint sprigs, to garnish

Peel and seed mangoes, then very thinly slice flesh.

Put mango slices in a bowl with chile, cashew nuts, raisins and chopped mint; stir gently. In a small bowl, mix together asafetida, cumin, cayenne and coriander; sprinkle over mango mixture.

Stir gently to coat mango mixture in spices, then cover and refrigerate 2 hours. Serve cold garnished with mint sprigs.

Makes about 2 cups.

LIME PICKLE

12 limes
¼ cup coarse sea salt
1 tablespoon fenugreek seeds
1 tablespoon mustard seeds
2 tablespoons chile powder
1 tablespoon ground turmeric
1 cup vegetable oil
Cilantro (fresh coriander) leaves, to garnish

Cut each lime lengthways into 8 thin wedges. Place in a large sterilized bowl, sprinkle with salt and set aside.

Put fenugreek and mustard seeds in a skillet and dry roast them over medium heat 1 to 2 minutes, until they begin to pop. Put them in a mortar and grind them to a fine powder with a pestle.

Add chile powder and turmeric and mix well. Sprinkle spice mixture over limes and stir gently. Pour over oil and cover with a dry cloth. Leave in a sunny place 10 to 12 days, until limes have been softened. Pack in sterilized jars, then seal and store in a cool, dark place. Serve at room temperature.

Makes about 6 cups.

VARIATION: To make lemon pickle, substitute 8 lemons for the limes.

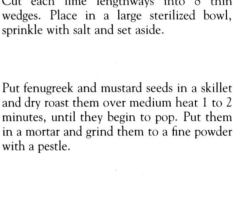

SAUTÉED CHILE PICKLE

2 teaspoons sesame seeds
1 teaspoon fennel seeds
2 teaspoons coriander seeds
2 teaspoons cumin seeds
¼ cup vegetable oil
½ teaspoon black peppercorns
20 fresh small green chiles
1 teaspoon mango powder
3 tablespoons lemon juice
Grated lemon peel, to garnish

Put sesame, fennel, coriander and cumin seeds in a skillet. Dry roast over medium heat, until spices begin to pop.

Add oil, peppercorns, chiles and mango powder and fry, stirring, 3 to 5 minutes, or until chiles are softened. Transfer to a serving dish, sprinkle with lemon juice and cool. Serve at room temperature, garnished with lemon peel.

Makes about 4 cups.

NOTE: For a less hot pickle, halve and seed chiles before cooking.

EGGPLANT PICKLE

1-½ lbs. baby eggplants
½ teaspoon ground turmeric
Salt to taste
2 cups vegetable oil
6 garlic cloves, crushed
1 (1-inch) piece fresh gingerroot, grated
1 tablespoon Garam Marsala, page 51
1 teaspoon red (cayenne) pepper

Cut eggplants in half lengthwise, sprinkle with turmeric and salt.

Heat 5 tablespoons of oil in a large skillet and fry eggplants about 5 minutes, until golden brown, stirring frequently. Stir in garlic and gingerroot and fry 2 minutes. Stir in Garam Masala, cayenne and remaining oil and cook, uncovered, 10 to 15 minutes, or until eggplants are soft, stirring occasionally.

Cool, then spoon into sterilized jars. Cover jars with a dry cloth 3 days, stirring gently every day. Seal jars and store in a cool, dark place. Serve at room temperature.

Makes about 4 cups.

NOTE: If baby eggplants are unavailable, use large eggplants and quarter lengthwise, then slice and prepare as above.

CUCUMBER RAITA

½ of large cucumber
1 cup plain yogurt
1 tablespoon chopped cilantro (fresh coriander)
1 tablespoon chopped fresh mint
1 green chile, seeded, finely chopped
Salt to taste
1 teaspoon cumin seeds
1 teaspoon mustard seeds
Cilantro (fresh coriander) or mint leaves, to garnish

CARROT & PISTACHIO RAITA

¼ cup coarsely chopped pistachios
⅓ cup raisins
6 tablespoons boiling water
4 carrots, coarsely grated
¾ cup plain yogurt
1 tablespoon chopped fresh mint
½ teaspoon chile powder
½ teaspoon cardamom seeds, crushed
½ teaspoon ground cumin
Salt to taste

Cut cucumber into matchstick-size pieces and place in a bowl. Add yogurt, cilantro, mint, chile and salt; stir gently to mix. Refrigerate 30 minutes.

Put pistachios and raisins in a small bowl and top with boiling water. Soak 30 minutes, then drain and pat dry with paper towels. Put carrots, yogurt, mint, chile powder, cardamom seeds, cumin and salt in a bowl and stir to mix.

Meanwhile, put cumin seeds and mustard seeds in a skillet and dry roast over medium heat 1 to 2 minutes, until they begin to pop. Cool, then sprinkle over the yogurt mixture. Cover and refrigerate 30 minutes. Serve cold, garnished with cilantro or mint leaves.

Makes about 1-½ cups.

Cover and refrigerate 30 minutes. Stir all but 2 tablespoons of pistachios and raisins into yogurt, then sprinkle remainder on top. Serve cold.

Makes about 1-½ cups.

VARIATION: Substitute chopped blanched almonds for pistachios.

FRESH MINT RELISH

CUCUMBER & CHILES

8 ounces fresh mint leaves, finely chopped
3 green chiles, seeded, finely chopped
1 small onion, finely chopped
1 (1-inch) piece fresh gingerroot, finely chopped
Salt to taste
2 teaspoons superfine sugar
2 tablespoons lemon juice
Mint leaves and lemon slices, to garnish

8 ounces cucumber
Salt to taste
2 green chiles, seeded, finely sliced
1 small fresh red chile, seeded, finely chopped
2 tablespoons white wine vinegar
1 teaspoon superfine sugar

Put mint leaves, chiles, onion and ginger-root in a bowl and mix thoroughly. Cover and refrigerate at least 1 hour.

Very thinly slice cucumber. Place in a colander and sprinkle with salt. Drain 30 minutes, then rinse thoroughly under cold running water. Pat dry with paper towels and arrange on a serving plate.

Stir in salt, sugar and lemon juice, mixing well. Serve cold, garnished with mint leaves and lemon slices.

VARIATION: Omit chiles and add 2 tablespoons chopped cilantro instead.

Sprinkle chiles over cucumber. Put vinegar and sugar in a small bowl and mix well. Sprinkle over cucumber, then cover and refrigerate 30 minutes. Serve cold.

NOTE: The chile seeds can be left in, if preferred, to make the dish very hot.

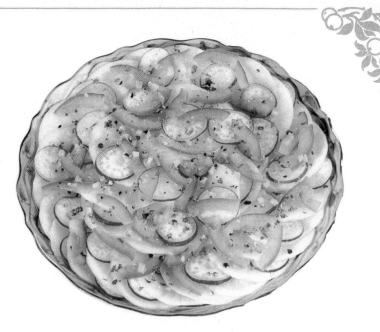

TOMATO KUCHUMBER

WHITE & RED RADISH SALAD

12 ounces cherry tomatoes
6 green onions
1 green chile, seeded, chopped
1 tablespoon lemon juice
Salt and red (cayenne) pepper to taste
2 tablespoons chopped cilantro (fresh coriander)
Green onions, to garnish

6 ounces white radish
10 red radishes
1 small green bell pepper
1 green chile, seeded, finely chopped
2 tablespoons lime juice
Salt to taste
6 black peppercorns, coarsely ground
1 tablespoon chopped fresh mint

Quarter tomatoes and put in a serving bowl. Cut onions diagonally into long, thin slices. Scatter onions and chile over tomatoes and gently mix together.

Peel and thinly slice white radish and slice red radishes. Arrange on a serving plate. Cut pepper into six pieces lengthwise, remove seeds and stem and slice finely. Scatter bell pepper and chile over radishes. Sprinkle salad with lime juice, salt, peppercorns and mint. Cover and refrigerate 30 minutes. Serve cold.

Makes 4 to 6 servings.

Sprinkle vegetables with lemon juice, salt, cayenne and cilantro, then cover and refrigerate 30 minutes. Serve cold, garnished with green onions.

Makes 4 to 6 servings.

VARIATION: Use larger tomatoes, if preferred, slice thinly and arrange on a serving plate. Scatter other ingredients over top, before chilling.

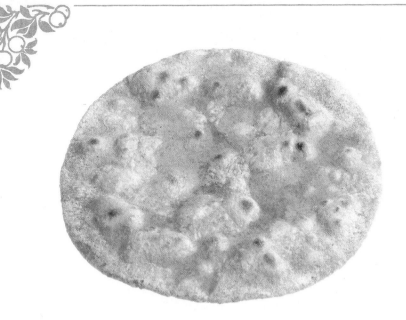

CHAPATI

1-¼ cups all-purpose flour
1-¼ cups whole-wheat flour
Salt to taste
About ¾ cup water
¼ cup butter or ghee, melted, plus extra for serving

Sift together flours and salt into a medium bowl, add any bran remaining in sifter. Mix in enough water to make a soft dough.

Knead dough on a lightly floured surface about 5 minutes, until smooth and pliable, then with wet hands, knead dough 1 minute more to make it extra smooth. Wrap in plastic wrap; refrigerate 30 minutes. Divide dough into 12 pieces and roll each out on a lightly floured surface to a 5-inch round.

Heat a griddle or heavy skillet over medium heat; cook rounds one at a time, floured side down, 1 to 2 minutes, until beginning to bubble on surface. Turn over and cook 30 to 60 seconds, pressing with a folded dry cloth during cooking to make them puff up. Wrap chapatis in a dry cloth as they are ready. Serve warm, brushed with extra melted butter.

Makes 12.

PIADINA

2-½ cups bread flour
1-¼ teaspoons salt
½ teaspoon baking powder
⅓ cup milk
⅓ cup water
3 tablespoons olive oil
TO SERVE:
Salami, cheese and salad

In a medium bowl, mix flour, salt and baking powder. In a measuring cup, combine milk and water. Add oil and a little of the water and milk mixture to flour mixture. Stir with a fork and gradually add more liquid until it has all been incorporated. Mix to form a soft dough.

Turn onto a lightly floured surface and knead until smooth. Cover and rest for 15 minutes. Divide dough into 12 equal pieces. Roll each piece out to a 3-inch circle.

Heat a heavy skillet or griddle until a drop of water flicked on the surface bounces and evaporates. Place 2 to 3 circles in skillet and cook 30 seconds. Flip over and continue cooking.

Turn each circle 2 or 3 times until sides are speckled with brown. Place on a wire rack while cooking remaining circles. Serve warm with salami, cheese and salad.

Makes 12.

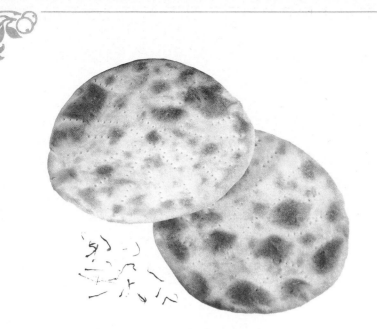

FLAKY OVEN BREAD

4 cups all-purpose flour
Salt to taste
½ cup butter or ghee, chilled
2 teaspoons superfine sugar
2 cups milk
Pinch of saffron threads

Sift together flour and salt into a medium bowl. Cut in all but 1 tablespoon of the butter, until mixture resembles coarse crumbs. Stir in sugar, then add about 1-¼ cups milk to make a soft dough.

Knead dough until smooth, then put into a clean, lightly oiled bowl. Cover and put in a cool place 2 hours. Put remaining milk in a small pan and heat until almost boiling, add saffron threads and let soak 1-½ to 2 hours. Preheat oven to 450F (230C); place a heavy baking sheet in oven to heat. Knead dough on a lightly floured surface and divide into 8 pieces. Roll 4 pieces at a time into balls, keeping rest covered with a dry cloth.

Flatten and roll first 4 balls out to 6-inch rounds. Prick all over with a fork. Press onto heated baking sheet in oven. Bake about 8 minutes, until beginning to brown, sprinkling rounds with a little saffron milk twice – without removing them from oven. Melt remaining butter or ghee and brush over breads, then sandwich them buttered sides together and wrap in a dry cloth while preparing remaining rounds. Serve warm.

Makes 8.

PARATHAS

½ cup all-purpose flour
⅔ cup whole-wheat flour
Salt to taste
½ teaspoon onion seeds
½ teaspoon celery seeds
About ⅔ cup water
1 cup butter or ghee, melted
Celery leaves, to garnish

Sift together flours and salt into a medium bowl; add any bran remaining in sifter. Stir in onion and celery seeds, then mix in enough water to form a fairly soft dough.

Knead dough on a lightly floured surface 5 minutes, or until pliable and smooth. Wrap in plastic wrap; refrigerate 30 minutes. Divide dough into 10 pieces and roll each out to a 5-inch round. Brush one side of each round with butter, then fold in half with buttered side inside. Brush top side with butter and fold in half again to make a triangle.

Roll out triangles on a lightly floured surface until both straight sides measure about 5 inches. Heat a griddle or heavy skillet and brush with butter. Cook 2 or 3 parathas at a time 1 minute, brush with butter, then turn over and cook 1 to 2 minutes more, until cooked. Stack on a plate, cover with a dry cloth while cooking remaining bread. Serve warm, garnished with celery leaves.

Makes 10.

POLENTA BREAD

1-⅓ cups coarse ground cornmeal
1 cup all-purpose flour
1-¼ teaspoons salt
¼ teaspoon pepper
3 tablespoons olive oil
1 cup lukewarm water
TO SERVE:
Salad

Preheat oven to 425F (220C). Grease a 12-inch pizza pan. In a medium bowl, mix together the cornmeal, flour, salt and pepper. In a small bowl, whisk together 2 tablespoons oil and water. Stir into the flour mixture with a fork to form a grainy paste.

Place in center of pan and press to edges with knuckles. Prick with a fork and brush with remaining oil. Bake 20 minutes until golden. Serve the bread warm with salad.

Makes 4 to 6 servings.

DOSA

⅓ cup urad dhal or brown lentils
1 cup long-grain rice
12 tablespoons water
2 green onions, finely chopped
2 tablespoons chopped cilantro (fresh coriander)
1 (1-inch) piece fresh gingerroot, grated
1 green chile, seeded, chopped
½ teaspoon salt
About 3 tablespoons water
Vegetable oil
Cilantro (fresh coriander) leaves, to garnish

Wash dhal and rice thoroughly; put into separate bowls. Add 2 cups water to each; soak 3 hours, then drain well.

Put dhal in a blender or food processor fitted with the metal blade. Add 6 tablespoons water and process until smooth. Puree rice with 6 tablespoons water in same way. Mix purees together in a large bowl, cover with a damp cloth and set aside at room temperature about 12 hours.

Stir in onions, coriander, gingerroot, chile, salt and enough water to make a thin batter. Heat a 6-inch skillet over high heat, brush with a little oil, then pour in 2 to 3 tablespoons batter and spread into a 4-inch circle. Cook about 3 minutes, until browned, turning over after about 1-½ minutes. Stack on a plate; cover with a dry cloth, while cooking remaining bread. Serve warm, garnished with cilantro leaves.

Makes about 12.

PIQUANT POPCORN

2 tablespoons corn oil
2 cloves garlic, crushed
1 (1/2-inch) piece gingerroot, peeled,
  chopped
1 cup popping corn
1/4 cup butter
2 teaspoons hot chili suace
2 tablespoons chopped fresh parsley
Salt to taste

Heat oil in a saucepan. Add 1 clove of crushed garlic, ginger and popping corn. Stir well.

Cover and cook over medium-high heat 3 to 5 minutes, holding lid firmly and shaking pan frequently until popping stops. Turn popped corn into a dish, discarding any unpopped corn kernels. Melt butter in pan. Stir in remaining clove of crushed garlic and chili sauce.

Return corn to pan and toss well until evenly coated with mixture. Add parsley and salt and stir well. Turn into a serving dish. Serve warm or cold.

Makes 6 to 8 servings.

Variation: Omit chili sauce and add 1 teaspoon dry mustard, 1 teaspoon paprika, 1/2 teaspoon ground coriander and 2 tablespoons chopped fresh chives to melted butter.

PEANUT BUTTER COOKIES

½ cup margarine, softened
½ cup crunchy peanut butter
½ cup granulated sugar
¾ cup light-brown sugar
1 egg, beaten
1-½ cups all-purpose flour
½ teaspoon baking powder
¾ teaspoon baking soda
Good pinch salt
½ teaspoon Mixed Spice, page 8
¼ teaspoon ground cinnamon
2 good pinches freshly grated nutmeg
Glacé cherry halves
Blanched almonds

Preheat oven to 375F (190C). Lightly grease 2 baking sheets. In a bowl, beat margarine, peanut butter, sugars and egg until well combined. Sift flour with baking powder, baking soda, salt and spices. Add to peanut butter mixture and mix well. Divide in 25 equal pieces and shape in balls. Place, spaced well apart, on greased baking sheets. Flatten to 2-inch circles by pressing several times with fork, first one way, then the other. Place a glacé cherry half in center of 13 cookies and almonds on remaining 12 cookies. Chill 30 minutes.

Bake cookies in preheated oven 10 to 12 minutes or until cooked through, but not hard. Cool on baking sheets 5 minutes, then remove to a wire rack to cool completely. Store in an airtight container up to 2 weeks.

Makes 25 cookies.

NOTE: These cookies should be slightly chewy in center. However, if you prefer them crisp, do not chill mixture.

ORANGE DRINK

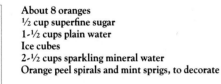

About 8 oranges
½ cup superfine sugar
1-½ cups plain water
Ice cubes
2-½ cups sparkling mineral water
Orange peel spirals and mint sprigs, to decorate

Squeeze juice from oranges to make 2-½ cups juice. Meanwhile, put sugar and plain water in a large saucepan; cook over a low heat, stirring occasionally, until sugar dissolves. Boil 5 minutes. Add orange juice and simmer another 5 minutes. Cool, then chill.

To serve, put ice cubes in glasses, add a little orange syrup, top with mineral water and decorate with orange peel and mint sprigs.

Makes about 5 cups.

NOTE: Use 2-½ cups commercial freshly squeezed orange juice, if preferred.

MILK & SAFFRON DRINK

½ teaspoon saffron threads
2 tablespoons boiling water
⅓ cup shelled pistachio nuts
Seeds from 10 green cardamom pods
¼ cup superfine sugar
5 cups cold milk
Crushed ice
¼ cup chopped pistachio nuts

Put saffron and boiling water in a small bowl; soak 30 minutes. Put in a blender or food processor fitted with the metal blade; add pistachio nuts, cardamom seeds and sugar. Process until smooth. Add milk and process until frothy.

Half-fill glasses with ice and pour in frothy milk mixture. Sprinkle with chopped pistachio nuts and serve at once.

Makes about 5 cups.

FRAGRANT LEMON DRINK

Grated peel and juice of 2 lemons
¼ cup superfine sugar
1 cup packed lemon balm leaves
Crushed ice
About 4 cups iced water
Lemon peel and lemon balm leaves, to decorate

Put lemon peel and juice, sugar and lemon balm leaves in a blender or food processor fitted with the metal blade; process until smooth. Strain into a pitcher and chill.

Fill glasses with crushed ice, add a little lemon concentrate and top with iced water, to taste. Serve at once, decorated with lemon peel and lemon balm leaves.

Makes about 5 cups.

NOTE: Lemon peel spirals: cut a long strip of peel from a lemon using a zester. Wind strip of peel around a skewer or chopstick, fasten securely to prevent it from unwinding and blanch in boiling water a few seconds. Rinse in cold water and remove skewer.

SPICED TEA

1 tablespoon plus 2 teaspoons black peppercorns
1 tablespoon cardamom seeds
1 tablespoon whole cloves
1 (1-½-inch) cinnamon stick
⅓ cup ground ginger
Hot tea
Boiling water
Milk and sugar to taste

Put peppercorns, cardamom seeds, cloves and cinnamon in a mortar and grind to a fine powder with a pestle. Add ginger and grind again a few seconds to mix. Add about ½ teaspoon of spice mixture to a pot of tea; leave in a warm place 1 to 2 minutes to brew. Serve hot, with milk and sugar.

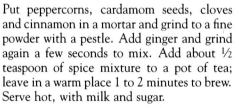

Makes about 8 tablespoons spice mix, enough for 16 pots of tea.

NOTE: Store remaining spice mixture in an airtight container, in a dark cupboard to preserve its flavor. It will keep 2 to 3 months.

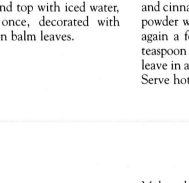

LIME & MINT DRINK

6 tablespoons lime juice
¼ cup superfine sugar
Pinch of salt
1 cup packed mint leaves
Ice cubes
About 4 cups iced water
Lime slices and mint leaves, to decorate

Pour lime juice into a blender or food processor fitted with the metal blade. Add sugar, salt and mint leaves; process until smooth. Strain into a pitcher, cover and refrigerate until cold.

Half-fill tall glasses with ice cubes; add a little lime juice concentrate and top with iced water to taste. Serve at once, decorated with lime slices and mint leaves.

Makes about 5 cups.

INDIAN SUMMER PUNCH

1 tablespoon fennel seeds
Seeds from 6 green cardamom pods
3 whole cloves
4 black peppercorns
½ cup ground almonds
¼ cup shelled pistachio nuts
½ cup shelled sunflower seeds
1-¼ cups boiling water
½ cup superfine sugar
3 cups cold milk
Apple slices and fennel sprigs, to decorate

Put fennel seeds, cardamom seeds, cloves and peppercorns in a mortar and grind to a fine powder with a pestle.

Put almonds, pistachios and sunflower seeds in a small bowl; add 6 tablespoons of the boiling water. Soak 20 minutes, the drain. Put in a blender or food processor fitted with the metal blade; add remaining boiling water and process until smooth.

Add spices and sugar; process again. Strain through a cheesecloth, squeezing paste to extract as much liquid as possible. Discard paste, cover and refrigerate liquid at least 1 hour, then mix with milk and serve in tall glasses over ice, decorated with apple slices and fennel sprigs.

Makes about 6 cups.

NOTE: If preferred, grind spices in a coffee grinder.

INDEX

Anchovy Spread 17
Apricot & Chicken Curry 58
Apricot Dessert 83
Austrian Chocolate Cup 48

Baklava 42
Barbecue Sauce 32
Barbecued Spareribs 16
Beef Satay 19
Berries with Pepper Sauce 40
Bombay Nut 'N' Raisin Mix 9
Brandy Snaps 44

Carrot & Pistachio Raita 86
Carrot Halva 78
Carrots with Fresh Dill 66
Cashew Nut Fudge 83
Ceylonese Chicken Curry 31
Chapati 89
Cheese Chile Bites 11
Cheesy Spanish Omelet 30
Cheesy Stuffed Tomatoes 70
Chicken Biriani 60
Chicken in Ginger Sauce 57
Chicken in Spicy Sauce 63
Chicken with Lentils 62
Chile Bean Tacos 24
Chile-Cheese Burgers 27
Chile Con Carne 28
Chile Pepper Pizza 29
Chilied Red Bean Dip 13
Chiles 6
Choc 'N' Spice Profiteroles 41
Cilantro & Chile Fish 73
Clam & Shrimp Chowder 25
Coconut Layer Cake 82
Coconut Milk 51
Coconut Pancakes 80
Cornish Saffron Cake 42
Creamy Saffron Fish Curry 76
Creole Gumbo Pot 15
Creole Jambalaya 26
Cucumber & Chiles 87
Cucumber Raita 86
Curried Chicken Liver Pâté 12
Curried Chicken Livers 63
Curried Garbanzo Beans 68
Curry Cream Mussels 19
Curry Powder 8

Deviled Crab Quiche 23

Deviled Tomatoes 14
Dosa 91
Duck & Coconut Curry 60
Duck with Honey & Lime 61

Eggplant Pickle 85
Eggplant Tahini Pâté 66

Falafel 31
Filo Shrimp Puffs 10
Fish in a Package 72
Fish in Hot Sauce 75
Five Spice Powder 8
Flaky Oven Bread 90
Fragrant Fried Rice 64
Fragrant Lemon Drink 94
Fresh Mango Chutney 84
Fresh Mint Relish 87
Fried Deviled Camembert 16
Frosted Gingerbread 43

Gado Gado 20
Garam Masala 8, 51
German Pepper Cookies 44
Ginger Beer 47
Glazed Apple Tart 40
Golden Semolina Pudding 81
Golden Steamed Chicken 61
Grilled Spiced Fish 77
Guacamole 17

Harissa 8
Hot Mulled Cider 46
Hot Mussels with Cumin 72
Hot Spice Mix 51

Iced Coffee Cream 79
Indian Fruit Salad 81
Indian Summer Punch 95
Indonesian Coconut Beef 29
Indonesian Coconut Sauce 34

Jamaican Chocolate Cake 43

Kashmir Meatball Curry 53

Lamb Korma 54
Lamb Tikka 53
Lamb with Cauliflower 56
Lamb with Onions 55
Lemon & Coriander Chicken 58

Lemon Butter Hollandaise 34
Lemon Ginger Syllabubs 39
Lentil-Stuffed Peppers 65
Lime & Mint Drink 95
Lime Pickle 84

Madras Meat Curry 54
Marinated Spiced Olives 9
Melon & Ginger Basket 39
Milk & Saffron Drink 93
Mixed Spice 8
Mixed Vegetable Curry 67
Moghul Masala 51
Moghul Shredded Duck 62
Mulligatawny Soup 18
Murghal Masala Chops 52
Mushroom Curry 69
Mussel & Saffron Soup 12
Mustard 6
Mustard Mozzarella Pork 23

Nasi Goreng 28
Negus 46
Nut Masala 51

Onion Bhajis 70
Orange Drink 93
Orange Ginger Duckling 21
Oriental Gingered Shrimp 14

Parathas 90
Peanut Butter Cookies 92
Pears in Pineapple Cream 38
Peppered Farmhouse Pâté 20
Peppered Salami Salad 37
Peppery Mozzarella Salad 71
Piadina 89
Piccalilli 36
Pickled Red Cabbage 37
Pickling Spice 8
Pina Colada Punch 45
Piquant Oriental Sauce 35
Piquant Popcorn 92
Pistachio Halva 78
Polenta Bread 91
Pork in Spinach Sauce 56

Roast Duck in Fruit Sauce 57
Roast Lamb & Pistachios 55
Roast Pepper Relish 35

Saffron Rice Pudding 80
Saffron Yogurt 79
Sautéed Chile Pickle 85
Scandinavian Fish Salad 77
Sesame Shrimp Toasts 18
Sherbert 47
Shrimp & Fish Ball Curry 76
Singapore Curry Puffs 22
Skewered Beef Kabobs 52
Snowy Flip 45
Sole with Dill Stuffing 73
Spice Mixes & Coconut Milk 51
Spice Mixtures 8
Spiced Brown Lentils 67
Spiced Melon Cocktail 13
Spiced Tea 94
Spices, A-Z 7
Spicy Beef Lettuce Cups 60
Spicy Chicken Patties 59
Spicy Garlic Fish Fry 74
Spicy Okra 71
Spicy Shrimp Patties 74
Spinach & Bean Dumplings 69
Steak Au Poivre 26
Steamed Fish & Vegetables 75
Stir-Fry Pork & Peppers 25
Stuffed Okra 65
Sweet Lassi 48
Sweet Saffron Rice 64
Sweet Spicy Chile Sauce 33

Tamil Nadu Vegetables 68
Tandoori Chicken 59
Tandoori Masala 51
Tangy Glazed Drumsticks 24
Tangy Mustard Sauce 33
Tangy Potted Cheese 11
Toasted Almond Toffee 82
Tomato Kuchumber 88
Tropical Fish Kebabs 21

Vegetable Couscous 27
Vegetarian Lentil Medley 30

White & Red Radish Salad 88
Wine & Pepper Cream Sauce 32
Wine Glazed Oranges 38

Yogurt Tomato Cooler 36